THE SECRET TO WINNING AN INTERNATIONAL SCHOLARSHIP

in 4 steps

First Edition

THE SECRET TO

WINNING AN

INTERNATIONAL

SCHOLARSHIP

IN 4 STEPS

First Edition

Tchetchet G. Digbohou

IES
InterEdu Solutions

Disclaimers

- Although every precaution has been taken in the preparation of this book, the publisher and author assume no responsibility for errors or omissions. Nor is any liability assumed for damages resulting from the use of the information contained herein.
- InterEdu Solutions LLC and the author make no representations or warranties with respect to the accuracy or completeness of the contents of the book
- The accuracy and completeness of the information provided herein and the opinions stated herein are not guaranteed or warranted to produce any particular results.

The Secret to Winning an International Scholarship

Bulk Sales
Discounted sales are available when ordered in quantity for bulk purchase or special sales in the U.S. and internationally.
For more information, please contact: sales@interedusolutions.com

Speaking engagements, workshops and, interview requests
For more information, please contact: prcontact@interedusolutions.com

THE SECRET TO WINNING AN INTERNATIONAL SCHOLARSHIP

IN 4 STEPS

FIRST EDITION

BY TCHETCHET G. DIGBOHOU

Pittsburgh, Pennsylvania USA

"Access to quality education has enabled me to reach far beyond the Bangladeshi village I grew up in"

Muhammad Yunus
Renowned social entrepreneur, founder of the Grameen Bank, and Nobel Peace Prize recipient for his pioneering role in the field of microfinance. As a student, Dr. Yunus received an international scholarship to study for a Ph.D. in economics in the U.S.

Content Overview

PREFACE: what this book is NOT about

ACKNOWLEDGMENTS   0

INTRODUCTION: 4 little, but yet resolute, steps   1

PART 1   **The landscape, the land mines, and the**   4
            landmarks: foundations for a successful start
- (International) scholarships explained
- The biggest hurdles you may ever face   5
- Where do you stand?   9
- The C-A-P-E® scholarship application process in a   12
  nutshell   15

PART 2   **Can you see clearly now?**   19
- Know thy self: clarity at all levels   20
- What are you looking for?   25
- Don't fall for this!   34
- The best tools in your (search) toolkit   37

PART 3   **A goldmine hiding in plain sight**   40
- Reading in between, behind and beyond the lines   40
- Secrets that should not be kept secret   46
- A note about study abroad programs   47

Part 4   **Rising up to the occasion**   49
- Moving from average to good   49
- Moving from good to great   58
- Moving from (great) potential to (great) delivery   58

Part 5   **It's not over until it's over**   61
- Flawless execution   61
- Am I on the right track?   63
- Now what?   64

FINAL THOUGHTS   68

RECOMMENDED READINGS (and other good resources)   69

APPENDIXES   72
- Appendix 1: international scholarship checklist   73
- Appendix 2: sample list of attributes in nationally competitive   74
  scholarships
- Appendix 3: examples of scholarships per host country/world   75
  region or per students' country of origin
- Appendix 4: good source for worldwide grade correspondence   97

PREFACE

What this book is NOT about

EVERY YEAR, BILLIONS OF DOLLARS IN THE FORM OF SCHOLARSHIPS, grants and various financial assistance are made available worldwide to help students and scholars partially or fully cover their higher education and research funding needs. Access to this funding is not unconditional. I suspect that if you are reading this guide today, it is most likely because you are thinking about applying for a scholarship or are seeking help so you can pursue schooling outside of your country of residence. Or maybe it is because you have already, unsuccessfully, applied for an international scholarship and are now probably asking yourself: "what did not work out?", "can I fix it?", "what are the true reasons for my failure?" or thinking "I am probably not as gifted as the other candidates." "I must have been unlucky." "How should I go about winning an international scholarship?"

In the vast print and online literature about domestic and international scholarship search and application, many authors seem to limit their "effort" to just listing sources for scholarships. If that is your expectations in picking up this manual, then I am afraid to say, it will not be of any use or benefit to you. Sadly, authors generally say very little about how to effectively look for, prepare and apply for those scholarships especially when it comes to the international ones. Just providing a listing of the sources for international scholarships would be of no significant value to prospective applicants. This book sets out to remedy the deficiencies in current literature and help demystify the whole scholarship search and application process. It walks you, the prospective applicant, through every step of the way. It is definitely NOT another database of scholarships but rather a coherent compilation of the best practices in international scholarship application. And even though this guide provides you with a list of some of the most common international scholarships in its appendix, we maintain that there is no such thing as a "magical" or "ready-to-use" list of academic or research scholarships.

.

The Secret to Winning an international Scholarship tries to answer two important questions:

- What scholarship is a "good fit" for you?
- How to successfully apply for the selected scholarship?

The ultimate goal is to provide you with reliable and simple tools to increase your likelihood of success.
It does so by using the intuitive step-by-step CAPE® method

ACKNOWLEDGMENTS

To LaShawn, for the treasure of love
To Nadre, for the daily inspiration

To Nancy Keteku and Angele Gnako for teaching me the basics of international educational advising.

This book would not have been possible without the great advice and editing of Dave Friede, Raven Neal, Archange Akenou, Andrew Pitrone and, Constant Ouapo.

To Kendria, Meiyi, Misti, Tiffany, Scott, Andy and, Sim aka Simiclaus;
To the University of Pittsburgh's Ed.D. cohort 2016; you truly are the new generation of adaptive leaders in education.

To all of you who have continuously encouraged and supported me;

To all of you who have relentlessly challenged me and sometimes counted me out, I must confess, you have been a blessing in disguise. Please, keep it up!

INTRODUCTION
4 little, but yet resolute, steps

NO MAGIC!

Our decade-long work as an International Educational Advisor has convinced us that successfully applying for study or research scholarships is not the result of sheer luck. To the contrary, winning international scholarships is almost always the result of a careful, rather lengthy and thoughtful process; it is the reward for a neatly put together strong and convincing application.
In their book "*The lucky few and the worthy many, scholarship competition and the world future leaders*", looking at the scholarship application process from a scholarship provider's perspective, the authors point out that competitive scholarship programs are generally seeking fifty specific attributes when calling for applicants, leaving no room for randomness. Such attributes include: ability to contribute to field of study, ability to contribute to society, adaptability, capacity for future influence, intellectual ability etc. (Read Appendix 2)

The cornerstone idea of this guide is that you can definitely increase your chances of winning an international scholarship if:

- You are committed to doing the "research" yourself
- You use a straight-forward method with straight-forward goals
- You pay close attention to the details of the applicants' selection process
- You show unmatched resolve and perseverance in your preparation
- You remain laser-focused on execution and on achieving your clearly stated goals

Demystifying (international) Scholarship Search and Application

This guide is an organized collection of advice and techniques directly coming from higher education specialists who have, throughout their careers, successfully assisted hundreds of scholarship applicants, or who have themselves been part of scholarship judging/awarding committees. It is the result of long and passionate work, interviewing, and observation.

This guide provides proven strategies, work habits, and practical steps you should be taking if you want to maximize your chances of being awarded an international scholarship. Here, the word "chance" is to be understood as "possibilities" or "potential".

My claim is bold: the act of applying for a scholarship can be broken up into a series of "events" you can influence and over which you can have control.

Don't get me wrong! I definitely do not want to promise scholarships to everybody because it would be not realistic or truthful. My ambition is to help explain, clarify and dig deeper into the process of applying for foreign scholarships. In so doing, I hope to help demystify the whole process and make you realize that there is nothing obscure or mysterious about it.

Our method consists in 4 letters: C-A-P-E

C – A – P - E® A 4-Step process in which each letter stands for:

C: Curiosity & Clarity
A: Analysis & Attention to detail
P: Preparation & Perseverance
E: Execution & Evaluation

CAPE® is our way of guiding international scholarship applicants towards success. I am confident it will show throughout the next few chapters.

ONE

ONE
The landscape, the land mines and, the landmarks: foundations for a successful start

"Every time you start doing something new, you will have standing up against you not just people who want to imitate you, but also those who want to emulate you, and most importantly you will have to face the vast majority of the ones who do not want to do anything but to keep discouraging you from taking any initiative." Confucius

After reading this chapter, you should be able to:
- Understand what is really meant by the term "scholarships" and by similar concepts
- Defeat negative preconceived notions about scholarships
- Understand the specifics of international scholarships
- Understand the premises of the CAPE approach

INTERNATIONAL SCHOLARSHIPS EXPLAINED: WHAT IS AN INTERNATIONAL SCHOLARSHIP?

What is a scholarship?
Generally speaking, a scholarship is partial or full financial or material support provided to a student or a researcher, allowing them to pursue schooling or research for a certain period of time. Scholarships can be provided either directly to the beneficiary through stipends and living/housing expenditure payment (or

reimbursements) or indirectly to the host institution through tuition payment.

The different types of scholarships
The term scholarship is typically used to describe 3 types of support provided to students and researchers:
- Scholarships (strictly speaking)
- Grants and subsidies
- Other financial and non-financial aids

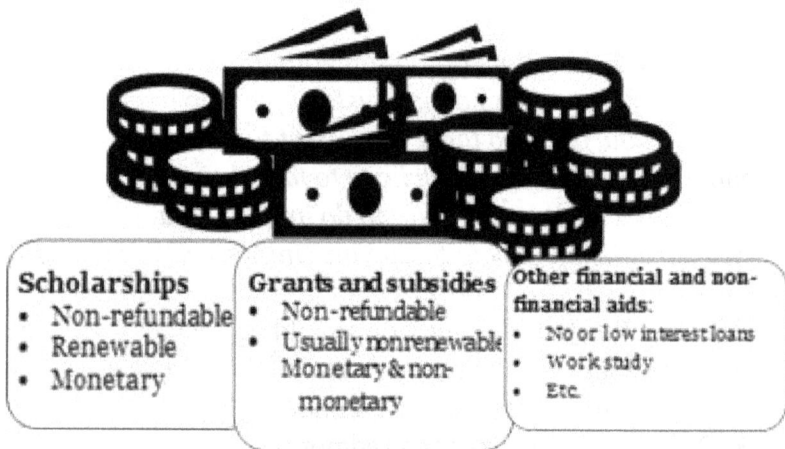

Scholarships	Grants and subsidies	Other financial and non-financial aids:
• Non-refundable	• Non-refundable	• No or low interest loans
• Renewable	• Usually nonrenewable	• Work study
• Monetary	Monetary & non-monetary	• Etc.

Fig. 1: The different categories of "scholarships"

Scholarships strictly speaking or classical scholarships
Scholarships are the commitment made by an organization/institution to pay, prepay, or reimburse all or part of a student's tuition or of any other academic or non-academic expenses. This payment is generally yearly, quarterly, or monthly-based. It could be renewable or non-renewable and is not indefinite. Some tuition discounts qualify as scholarship.

Grants and subsidies
This is non-reimbursable financial assistance or aid. It is a set amount generally paid to the beneficiary once. Under certain circumstances, some subsidies or grants can be renewed or

extended. In practice, the line between grants and material aid could be blurred.

Other financial and non-financial aids
Material aids and various non-financial support
This category refers to in-kind (material or intellectual) support. For example: an academic or research institution which provides at no charge a key piece of equipment that is central to the beneficiary's work. Providing airfare tickets so the beneficiary can attend an important scientific colloquium or conference. Waiving credit hours based on the applicant's previous academic accomplishments. All of which translate into lower tuition overall.

Other associated concepts
Many types of aids do not meet the definitions outlined in the above paragraphs to the letter. They nevertheless significantly alleviate students' financial and material burden. They are namely interest free, low interest or heavily subsidized student loans. Work study opportunities for students is also an example.

What is an international scholarship?
The term "international scholarship" refers to any scholarship or nonrefundable aid obtained by a student outside of their country of origin, residence, or citizenship. By extension, an international scholarship can also refer to a scholarship received by a student from an institution located in his or her country of origin in order to pursue schooling overseas. International scholarships are often "opposed" or "compared" to "local" or "national" ones. At its core, an international scholarship is not very different from a so-called "local" or "domestic" one when it comes to the type of support provided. The main difference resides not in the nature of the aid but rather in the way applicants go about finding out about and applying for them. Indeed, international scholarships require a more complex and refined "detection/research" and application approach. It goes without saying that most techniques offered in this book are also applicable to "local" scholarships.

7

Applying for an international scholarship is in many ways similar to applying for a domestic one. For example, in both cases, the applicant must adhere to a comprehensive set of requirements more or less spelled out by the scholarship provider and go through a selection and award process. However, despite those similarities, domestic and international scholarship applications differ in many other ways. For example, applying for an international scholarship additionally requires that applicants display a set of specific aptitudes. Amongst those aptitudes are, for example, the capacity to project one's self into a social and academic culture or into a language which is not originally theirs. Therefore, international scholarship applicants need to be prepared to face, on top of standard and expected scholarship requirements, multiple level of obstacles which might make the whole search and application process even more grueling and challenging.

Full international scholarship awards are typically made up of:

Core components
- Tuition (or composition fee)
- Stipend for one student (maintenance allowance)
- One round-trip airfare
- Student/scholar visa and administrative costs

Additional or discretionary components
- Family allowance (spouse, children, etc.)
- Research and capacity building funding
- Hardship funding for unforeseen difficulties

Costs of scientific equipment or comparable academic resources are usually not covered.

THE BIGGEST HURDLES YOU MAY EVER FACE

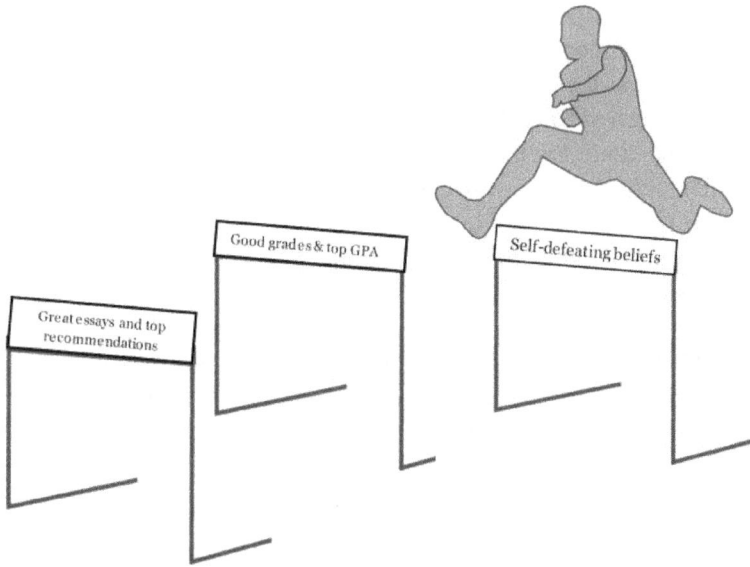

Fig 2: the scholarship hurdle race.

The scholarship hurdle race: be prepared to jump over every single hurdle

Before you get started with applying for an international scholarship, be aware that one of the biggest hurdles that may impede your progression resides inside of you and in your immediate environment. Amongst those obstacles are, for example, deeply seeded self-doubt, unjustified preconceived ideas about the scholarship application process and misunderstandings of what is expected of you throughout that process. Unfortunately, too many students, just like you, may have raised barriers in their own minds. Those barriers are made up of nearly indestructible certitudes which over the years have become mental "concrete walls" preventing you from applying with a clear mind.

9

The most popular preconceived notions about scholarship in general and about international scholarships in particular
Why you need to be aware of them
"Scholarships are very rare and way too hard to get"
"Getting a scholarship involves too much work and it is too complicated, I will never make it happen!"
"The scholarship awarding process is generally not very transparent"
"The scholarship application "game" is always rigged because the winners are always known in advance"
"If you don't know an insider or someone involved in the scholarship award process, you will never be selected"
"Winning a scholarship is exclusively reserved to the top of the class, super genius or to those with very high IQ"
"Winning a scholarship is only for the elite"
"Winning a scholarship is a matter of luck. It is just like gambling"
"Winning a scholarship is too late for me. It's passed my age and I do not meet the degree requirement"

Why you need to dispel the myths about international scholarships
"Winning an international scholarship is a matter of luck. It's like playing the lottery"
FALSE! This statement summarizes a false but apparently widespread idea. I concede that our occasional usage of the word "winning" throughout this guide may contribute to establish the notion that applying for an international scholarship is just like playing the lottery or gambling. Throughout this guide, we will be deliberately also using the terms "to obtain", "to successfully apply for", and "to be the beneficiary of".
"You need to be an insider or to know someone in the scholarship committee in order to successfully apply for an international scholarship"
FALSE! This is far from being an isolated comment, as I have heard it countless times during my public presentations. It embodies a solidly rooted preconceived notion: it's not about

what you know but rather who you know. Here again, our experience shows that there is no need to personally know people in "high places" for your scholarship application to be successful. Unfortunately, way too many talented students get into the scholarship search and application process already resigned and defeated. The outcome of their applications is therefore unsurprisingly "failure".

For some, the origin of that pessimistic attitude can be traced back to the social or political environment they are "trapped" in. An environment where most scholarship award processes are opaque and where the most abject forms of nepotism, corrupted networking and unfair practices rule supreme. Many students don't dare to take the leap. They no longer want to put the effort into searching and smartly applying for (international) scholarships.

Throughout the years, it has personally been reported to us that in many countries, access to scholarships and non-refundable financial aid is almost exclusively reserved for non-meriting students; for students with family connections; for students with no significant financial needs. All while students in need of financial support or with strong academic records are ignored or left behind. It is a shame! I firmly denounce this unfairness! The defeatist attitude of many students is certainly understandable but cannot justify resignation or lack of persistence. Know that international scholarships are also within your reach provided you are curious about understanding the method to do it successfully and you commit to putting in the attention and time. This book has been written to help you do just that.

"Scholarships are only for geniuses and for students with excellent grades"
FALSE! OR... NOT QUITE RIGHT...
Granted, winning scholarships is a very competitive and demanding process. Being a high-achieving student with very good grades gives any scholarship applicants an undeniable leg up on the competition. This goes without saying! ...Top grades, honor rolls and awards are definite assets to hold when applying for international scholarships or for any scholarship, for that

matter. But keep in mind that competing for an international scholarship is not just about having a perfect or a high Grade Point Average (GPA) (Appendix 4), but it is also about "scoring" high on a variety of many other factors which could prove to be just as key. You should also make sure to emphasize your many other strengths (extracurricular, leadership, professional expertise, etc.) and pay attention to the way you present yourself when given the opportunity in your application via your essays, personal statement, study objective statements or interviews... It is therefore not always mandatory to have earned top grades or to have a perfect GPA in order to obtain a scholarship, but it helps to have good academic records...

Although most of the above-listed preconceived notions are baseless, they do unfortunately slow down or greatly damper students' drive. It is perfectly fine to be aware of them but I would strongly urge you "to get over" them without a single regret. Don't be defeated. Do not allow your mind to get overburdened by them.

The first challenge you must overcome is getting rid of deeply rooted negative preconceived notions so they don't keep you away from an otherwise very achievable goal: winning a scholarship...

WHERE DO YOU STAND?

Merit-based vs. need-based scholarships
Scholarships generally fall into three arbitrary categories based on the underlying philosophy of the provider.

Scholarships are said to be:
- **Strictly merit-based** when the providers seek to attract applicants with high academic achievements and strong leadership track records or potential. They are also known as need-blind scholarships.
- **Strictly need-based** when they cater to prospective applicants of modest or no financial means, from specific countries or social groups, or from historically disadvantaged communities. Through the application

paperwork, scholarship providers are able to assess the level of needs of applicants.

- **Any combination of both merit and need-based**.

In reality, given the high volume of applications in regard to the number of awards available, most need-based scholarship contests turn into merit-based races. Many scholarship providers would (logically) rather reward the highest academic achievers amongst applicants with financial needs.

The merit-based/need-based quadrant

Depending on the unique combination of such factors as financial needs (need-based) or academic performance and leadership (merit-based), students range from high-achieving/financially-deprived to low-achieving/financially-self-sufficient and any nuances in-between. In reality, those combinations are not hermetically separated from one another. They overlap and end up forming a continuum. It is therefore more accurate to speak of the merit-based/need-based spectrum. For the sake of clarity, educational advisors generally define four categories of potential scholarship applicants illustrated in the merit-based/need-based quadrant (Fig. 3).

Briefly think of your own current situation. What are you going to lean on when considering applying? Your "merits", your needs or both? Can you determine where you stand today by taking a close look at the following graph?

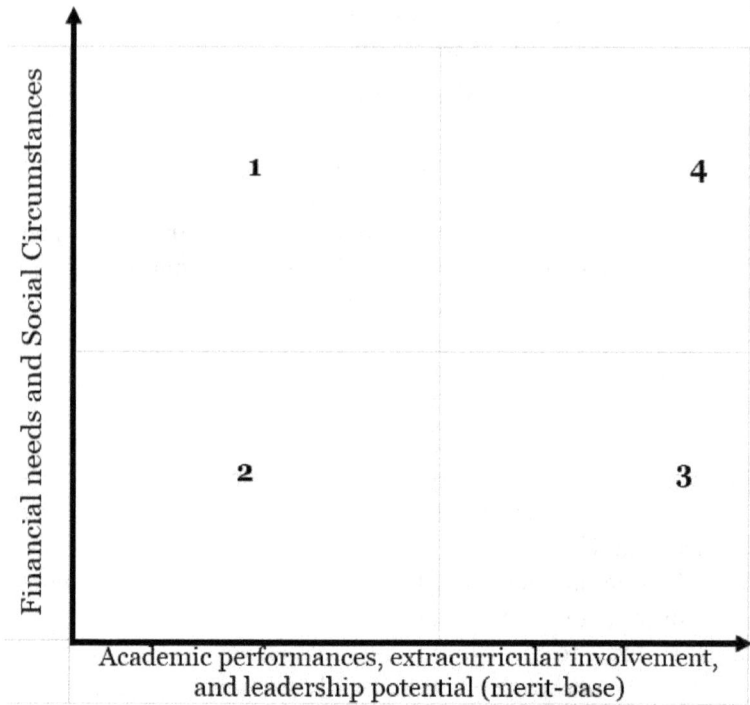

Fig 3: The merit-based/need-based quadrant

Understanding the merit-based/need-based quadrant

- Area 1. This area includes students with low academic performance, low extracurricular involvement, and leadership potential but with significant financial needs
- Area 2. This area includes students with low academic performance and no extracurricular accomplishments but also without any significant financial needs
- Area 3. This area includes students with top academic achievements and strong leadership potential but showing no major financial needs or adverse social circumstances
- Area 4. In this area are students with high academic performance, great leadership potential but displaying significant financial needs

The truth is, from a merit-based scholarship judge's perspective or even more broadly speaking, from a school admission officer's standpoint, the most "attractive" applicants are the ones assessed to belong to Area #3: the students with strong academic records, leadership potential but displaying no significant financial needs. From a need-based scholarship provider's perspective though, the most "attractive" applicants are the ones assessed to belong to Area #4: the top achievers with promising leadership potential but showing significant financial needs or facing difficult social circumstances.

What quadrant of the graph are you in?

By defining your personal profile and "tidying" the various levels of "requirements and selection criteria"(read Part 3), you should be able to determine more accurately what still remains for you to do in order to bridge the gap between your situation today and where you need to be.

THE C-A-P-E® SCHOLARSHIP APPLICATION PROCESS IN A NUTSHELL

Postulate

For a smooth and successful implementation of the method described in this guide and for practical reasons, we have made some basic assumptions. Those suppositions led to the following postulate about you, the would-be applicant:

- You are in high school, a college/university student, a researcher, or you have been one in the recent past.
- You graduated high school (or are on track to doing so) or you hold a college degree or college-level certificate.
- You have a cumulative GPA of at least 2.50 (Read Appendix 4 for corresponding worldwide grades or marks)
- You have a near fluent knowledge of one of the major world languages and you also possess basic knowledge of the English language or are firmly committed to doing everything possible to gain advanced knowledge of English. Most international programs post their information and application materials in the major language of the country or the region where they are

located; the academic part is also conducted in that language. It is however important to point out that an increasing number of those scholarship program statements is also available online and in English. If by the time you are considering applying for a scholarship you do not speak the regional or country language, English might, in many instances, give you the opportunity to access the preliminary information about a scholarship program.

- You have public or private access to the internet and are quite familiar with surfing the web and using the internet, or you are firmly committed to getting familiar with those tools.

- You are willing to "get your hands dirty" by personally following through each and every one of the steps described in this guide.

- You have demonstrated interest in areas beyond schooling and you are involved in extracurricular activities: socio-cultural, sports, leadership at large, etc.

- You are very eager to learn and are not afraid of challenges.

- You have read and reread the previous section about "preconceived notions". Seriously!

If you are applying as a researcher, the following items should be added to the above list:

- You are currently working as a faculty member or researcher, or you have held such positions or similar ones in the recent past.

- You have performed (individually or as part of a team) research or research-related work. This work is ongoing, completed or still relevant.

- There have been articles, theses, or papers written or published (by you or others) about your work or your specialized field of interest.

BRIEF DESCRIPTION OF THE 4-STEP CAPE PROCESS
The CAPE approach revolves around 4 key ideas summarized in a 4-letter acronym: CAPE

C-A-P-E stands for:

C: Clarity and Curiosity
A: Analysis and Attention to details
P: Preparation and Perseverance
E: Execution and Evaluation

CAPE® can be summarized as follows:
"This is how other students before you have put together winning applications" or
"This is how to go about convincing the people who make the scholarship award decision (scholarship judges) that you deserve one" or
"This is how to maximize your chances of being awarded an international scholarship"

Each letter of this acronym represents a key attribute any applicant must have in order to increase their chances to win an international scholarship. Each letter also represents a set of proven techniques any candidate must understand and faithfully apply.

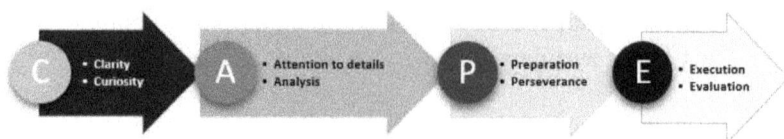

| C • Clarity • Curiosity | A • Attention to details • Analysis | P • Preparation • Perseverance | E • Execution • Evaluation |

• How to plan and organize for an effective search • How to define your personal, academic, and professional profile • How to clarify your objectives • How and what to search for • Where to search for scholarships • How to avoid frauds • How to start thinking like a scholarship provider • How to effectively use scholarship search tools	• How read scholarship application requirements • How to read in between the criteria statement lines • How to narrow down your initial selection • How to assess your current strengths and weaknesses	• What to prepare for • How to get ready to meet the requirements • How to write outstanding essays	• How to meet all the deadlines • How prepare for plan B
Search Phase	**Planning Phase**	**Preparation Phase**	**Application Phase**

Fig 4: CAPE Scholarship application process

The following chapters will illustrate:

- How important it is for you to get familiar with the scholarship application requirements and with the broader context of scholarships
- How to successfully use a quasi-scientific but yet very intuitive search and application method

TWO

Two
Can you see clearly now?
C for Clarity, C for Curiosity

"When I was in college, I wanted to be involved in things that would change the world."
Elon Musk: South African-born innovator and industrialist; earned a full scholarship to the University of Pennsylvania in 1992

After reading this chapter, you should be able to:
- Use effective organizing tools for better planning
- Clearly define your personal and academic profile
- Thoroughly search for and select the scholarships that are right for you (what to look for, where and how to do so)

AS PROSPECTIVE INTERNATIONAL SCHOLARSHIP APPLICANTS, you must demonstrate clarity both personally and when it comes to setting your goals early on in the process. You should also demonstrate unshakable curiosity.

KNOW THY SELF: CLARITY AT ALL LEVELS
Here are some questions to consider as you delve into the need for clarity:
- How is your scholarship search organized?
- What is your personal profile? What are your personal, academic, and professional goals and objectives?
- How are you actually going to go about searching and selecting the scholarship to apply for?

Beware! Untidiness and lack of organization in your scholarship pursuit could be one of your worst "enemies" throughout the process. You should strive to be well organized and methodological from the get go. If you are not meticulous, I can guarantee that the entire process will be chaotic, rambling, and confusing... Confusion and chaos could be major impediments to your efforts and may potentially bring your quest to a halt. As a result, you may feel discouraged. Avoid disorganization as much as possible!

Build and use a monthly or weekly calendar or schedule (whether paper or electronic) where you will list and carefully keep track of the actions which need to be taken, the progress you have accomplished along the way, and the key milestones and potential hurdles to overcome. If you opt for an electronic calendar, use such popular electronic tools as Outlook or Google Calendar and draw a time line. The search for international scholarships is an intensive everyday effort. You must be proactive and make sure to take specific actions that would get you closer to your goal of securing a scholarship. I recommend that you get started with your scholarship search very early on. Start at least 18 to 24 months before the date you anticipate beginning school overseas (Read Part 3).

Setting the groundwork for successful scholarship search and application

The starting point of any successful international scholarship search and application is clarity and uncompromising honesty when describing your personal, academic and professional profile. Before you rush to fill out scholarship application forms hurriedly printed off the internet or handed over to you by a foreign embassy receptionist, I strongly recommend that you lay out your "personal profile" in writing. This step and the ones that follow, namely the collecting, sorting out, and usage of relevant information, must be carried out in an orderly and very purposeful manner. You might find it unnecessary and think, "I already know who I am, why waste time writing it down?" Think again!

This is not quite drafting your resume or curriculum vitae but rather a detailed self-identification sheet. This step consists of answering with precision open-ended questions, providing honest answers to questions relating to your achievements, academic and professional career choices.

21

Such questions as:

- What have I achieved (personally, professionally, and academically) so far?
- What are my academic, personal and professional goals?
- What job would I like to do in the 3 to 5 years following graduation?
- What are my motivations for wanting to do that job or be in that professional field?
- What can I fundamentally and uniquely bring to my community, to my country, and to the world?

You must draft your profile very patiently. The next pages explain how. This step is meant to help you lay the groundwork for your scholarship search. Defining your personal profile in writing is therefore not optional.

"Who am I?" Who am I: how to define your personal, academic, and professional profile.

The following table recapitulates the areas your profile should cover and provides a sample of the type of questions to ask yourself.

Broad questions	Specific questions
Who am I	• State my name, age, gender • State my current job title and occupation • State my most relevant and past job titles and occupations as well as internships • State any voluntary and unpaid job I have held
What have I achieved so far?	• List my most recent degree • List all the degrees I have earned (without exception) the highest, past and most recent ones • List of my professional certificates • List all other academic or nonacademic credentials I hold • List all the honors and distinctions I have received • List all scholarships, awards, trophy I have received in any capacity so far • List all the tests and exam I have passed • List all my major personal, professional and, academic achievements • List all the organizations I have played an active role in • List all my leadership achievements • State why you have a leadership potential? • Provide specific examples • Give my specific future goals
How involved am I my community?	List my most significant community service activities or civic involvement
What are my specific academic objectives?	What degree/certificate would I like to earn in the next 3 to 5 years? (Please use scenario provided in the following section and in Fig.6)
What are my specific professional objectives?	What profession (or professional fields) would I like to be in the next 3 to 5 years? (Please use scenario provided in Fig.6)

Fig 5: "Who am I?" Defining your profile

When "objectively" defined, your profile should help you:

● Improve your search through key word refinement: determining the words that are the most important to your study, research, and profession; the key words that are going to be the foundation for your scholarship search

- Define the different study paths and possible career scenarios open to you
- Generate the ingredients for drafting powerful essays
- Produce the building blocks for drafting strong and thoughtful recommendation letters

How to continue to enrich your profile

You are strongly encouraged to continue to enrich, modify and adapt your general and personal profile as needed throughout the scholarship search and application process by coming up with two to four possible academic and professional scenarios for yourself that lay out paths that you could potentially take... Following is an example of how to expand on the answer to "what are your professional objectives?"

- First, starting with a given professional objective, you are encouraged to come up with at least 3 other related potential professions.
- Secondly, on your own or with the help of an educational adviser, find out 2 or more possible fields of study which are likely to lead up to the career you have previously identified. Keep an open mind, and be imaginative and creative.

You will find out that it is in theory possible to list at least 6 fields of study that are likely to lead up to the professions and careers you may be thinking about entering.

Let's be realistic, not all of those fields may be the perfect or ideal ones you are probably thinking about at the moment, but they should be the closest possible. They should allow you to broaden your international scholarship search base. A wide enough search base is also an asset when it comes to deciding which countries or programs to target.

24

How to expand your possible fields of study and your scholarship search

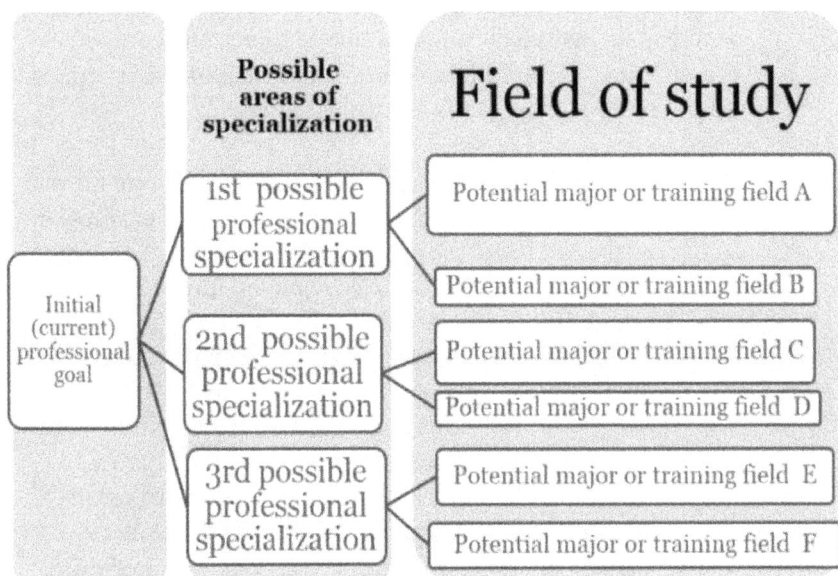

Fig 6: Professional scenario path

WHAT ARE YOU LOOKING FOR?
C FOR CURIOSITY: SHOWING LIMITLESS CURIOSITY

Curiosity is not just a mental attitude but more importantly a series of specific actions to be taken. Those actions are translated into everyday deeds or accomplishments of your desire to search extensively yet smartly. A student once described to me how, when he was considering applying for a scholarship, he was consumed by a nearly obsessional yet orderly form of curiosity. Most scholarship programs are set up by universities, foundations, governments, public agencies, public or private companies, or multilateral regional institutions. You should be curious, for example, about the backgrounds and the real motivations of scholarship providers. In other words, curiosity to understand the true reasons why any given scholarship program exists in the first place.

Understanding why scholarship programs exist in the first place

Without getting into lengthy socio-philosophical considerations, we estimate that most countries, foundations, and companies that initiate, set up, facilitate or manage scholarship programs, do so because of one of the following reasons:

- To ATTRACT TALENTED PEOPLE in multiple fields from around the world to the country or institution. For example, in order to attract the best athletes into their programs, many universities set up scholarship funds. For example, in the U.S., Fairleigh Dickinson University, just as many other universities, set up a scholarship program aimed at recruiting talented soccer player students. In France, the International Center for Cancer Research offers research scholarships and post-doctorate funding in order to attract the best researchers on cancer regardless of nationality into their network of research centers.
- To PROMOTE CULTURAL AND ACADEMIC EXCHANGE worldwide. For example, the German government offers through DAAD (The German Academic Exchange Service) scholarship to students and researchers from around the globe seeking to pursue schooling or conduct research in Germany.
- To PROMOTE REGIONAL COOPERATION. For example, in Africa, the Economic Community of West African States (ECOWAS) has set up a scholarship program open to citizens of all 15-member countries. In Europe, the Erasmus program has been set up by the European Union member countries to benefit students looking for schooling opportunities anywhere in the EU territory. Each region and sub-economic or economic region of the world, without a single exception has set up one or multiple programs aimed at funding schooling and research regionally or internationally for its citizens.
- To ENSURE THE POLITICAL, CULTURAL OR EVEN RELIGIOUS INFLUENCE of a country. For example, the government of Qatar offers scholarships to non-Qatari students in order to

promote their political and diplomatic vision of the world. Another example is the one of "emerging" political and economic "powers". Some of which are increasingly setting up generous scholarship packages targeted at international students and researchers in order to attract them into their best universities. The most striking example is the BRICS: Brazil, Russia, India, China, and South Africa. While many students would exclusively look for scholarship opportunities in a handful of Western countries, they unknowingly ignore a growing number of high value scholarship opportunities available around the world, not just in the western hemisphere.

- To PROMOTE AN ORGANIZATION OR A COMPANY'S IDEALS, PHILOSOPHY AND AGENDA. For example, countless organizations such as the Coca Cola Foundation, the Mo Ibrahim Foundation or the Rotary International offer a very diverse array of international scholarship programs promoting their respective institutional missions and goals. That may also include emphasizing a charitable mission. For example, the Aga Khan International Scholarship Program was initiated by the Aga Khan Development Network (AKDN) a nonprofit organization which is involved in promoting benevolent childhood education and health as well as lifelong learning for adult.

- To PROMOTE A SPECIFIC FIELD OF STUDY OR RESEARCH AND TO ADVOCATE FOR A PARTICULAR OCCUPATION. For example, AACE International, the International Association of Cost Engineers, offers an international scholarship for current or future professionals in the field of cost engineering.

Being able to understand the mindset, the true motivations behind international scholarships and the stated goals of the scholarship providers is one of the keys to your success. The need to understand that mindset must be stronger than any urge you may have to quickly fill out application forms.

Why do scholarships X, Y and Z exist?

What is their stated and sometimes "hidden" mission and agenda?

When were they created?

What do the alumni of scholarships X, Y and Z say about the programs and about their own experience?

What do the alumni have in common?

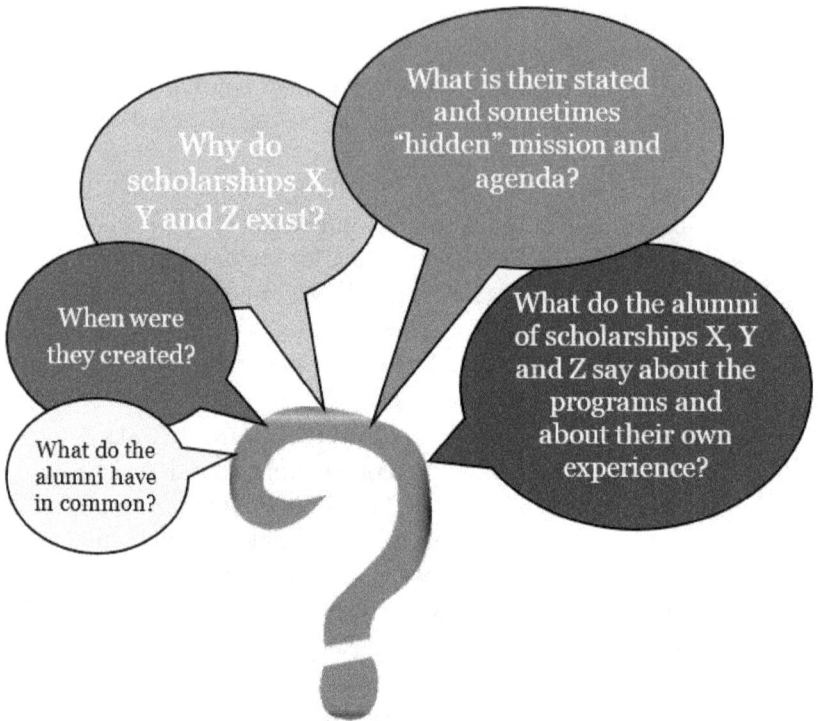

Fig 7: Questions to ask yourself very early in the process

Where and how to search: physical, online/electronic, and other search techniques Scholarship searches are performed both physically and electronically.

Physical search: make sure to thoroughly explore your immediate environment and collect as much information and documentation as possible...

- Ask your student advisor at your school or at your local college
- Ask your local or school librarian
- Visit embassies, cultural centers, local foundations or international organizations that are dedicated to the promotion of education, social or research-related issues
- Reach out to local representatives of multinational companies
- Reach out to local representatives of non-governmental organizations
- Make sure to visit embassies and organizations in person
- Take part in any relevant informational sessions and ask as many questions as possible and carefully take notes

Electronic search: a significant portion of your scholarship information search is to be done online using Google and other reputable specialized web search engines. Part 3 explains in detail what information to look for.

Depending on your country of residence, the search engines may vary. For example, in China Baidu or Sogu are probably going to be more relevant. For the sake of simplicity and effectiveness, our advice will essentially be about Google.com, the world's top search engine.

EFFECTIVELY USING GOOGLE IN YOUR INFORMATION SEARCH
The following is a list of tips that will help you effectively conduct your information search using Google

- Use words that are very specific and relevant to the topic of scholarship (i.e. university scholarship, international scholarship).
- Avoid vague or ambiguous words.
- Look for and use synonyms. Ex: foreign scholarship, university financial aid.
- Use a maximum of 2 to 4 key words at a time; preferably in English.
- Make sure to avoid using articles, pronouns or verbs, and other very common words
- Avoid using such punctuations as commas (,) and question marks (?).

For example, if you are looking for scholarships to study in China in the field of business administration, here are some of the key words you could use in your online search:

china scholarship international student (create illustration in Word meeting pixel quality criteria)

- Search once using generic or basic words and search again using words that are directly derived from each of the generic words you initially used. I.e. engineer (generic) vs engineering (derivative).

- Sometimes, feel free to go beyond the first results page. Since search engines tend to list the most relevant results on the first page, do not hesitate to go beyond that first page of results.
- Recombine your key word order. It is recommended to tweak your initial keywords and check if you are getting more or different search results. Do not hesitate to search by inverting the key words or by replacing one or two words by others that are more precise.

The following are examples of Google search results generated by either a recombination, an addition, a slight modification, or an inversion of keywords:

Keywords option 1: china scholarships international student
Keywords option 2: china international students scholarship
Keywords option 3: scholarship china foreign student
Keywords option 4: china business international scholarships
Keywords option 5: china government business international scholarships

Search results for:
China scholarships international student

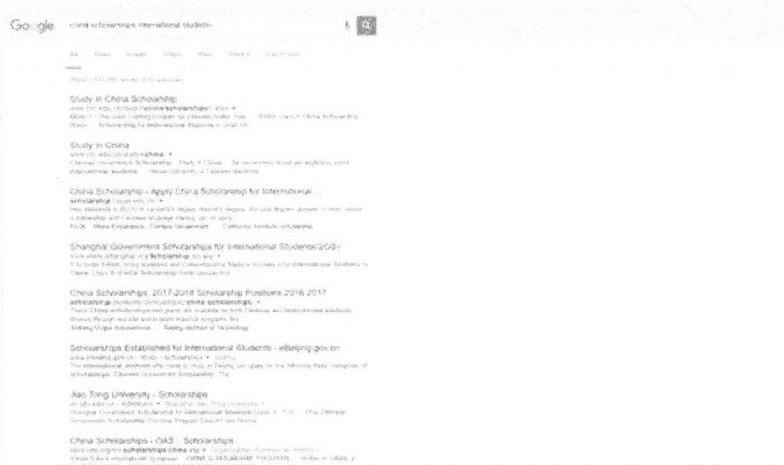

Search results for:
China international students' scholarship

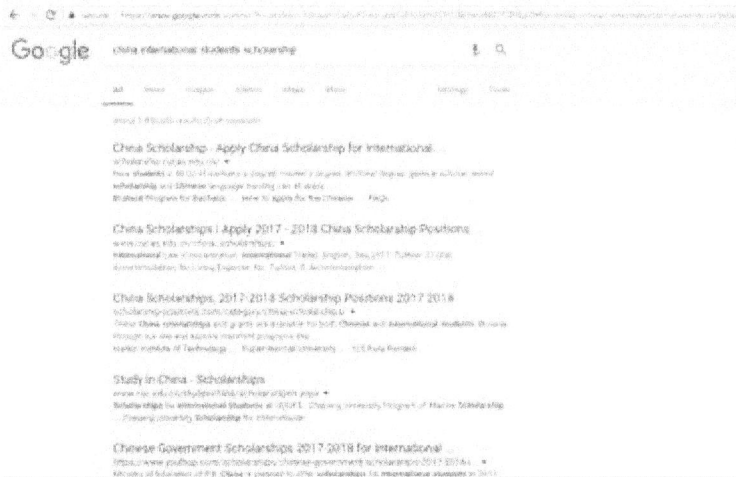

Search results for:
scholarship china foreign student

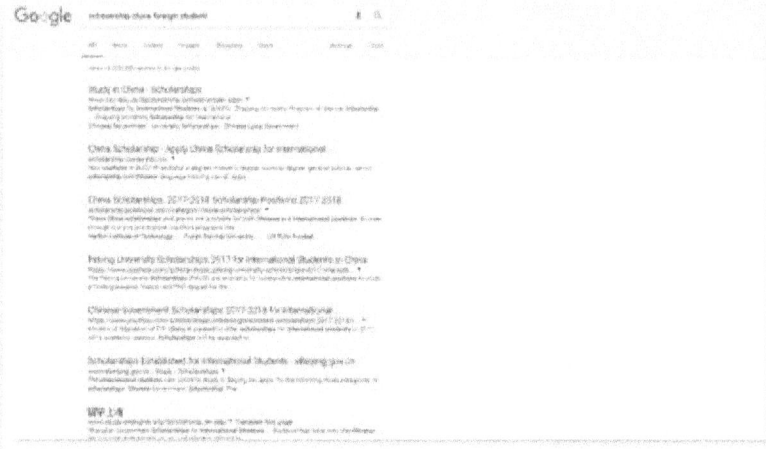

- Use quotation marks. Quotation marks allow you to limit the search results to the exact wording used

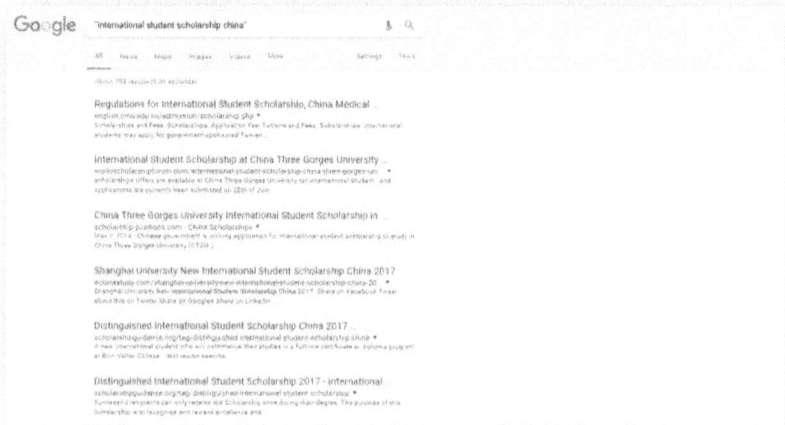

- Perform an intra search. After the general Google search, it is strongly recommended to do an "intra" search. An intra search is a search conducted within the website of the relevant result landing page if it exists. Make sure to use more specific words for the intra search

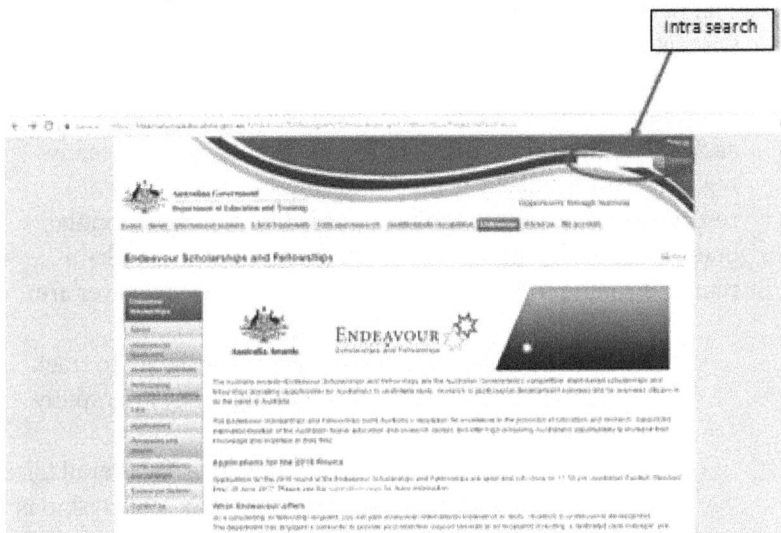

Fig 8: Google intra search

- Use Google alerts and scholarship apps

You can also set a Google alert - a way for you to get automatic emails about scholarship-relevant topics, by following the 7 steps below:

- Go to Google Alerts on the Google landing page.
- In the box at the top, enter topic or scholarship relevant key words.
- Choose how frequently you wish to receive notifications.
- Set the language and world region you wish to get alerts from.
- Set the number of results you want to receive.
- Complete the alert setting. Voila!!!

The Google search engine will scour the web, pull "data" that contains and matches the key words you have entered and email the result to you.

A noticeable downside of Google alerts is that your mailbox may overflow with inaccurate or redundant information. Some argue that parsing through this type of bulk data might not always be a wise use of your time.

Many also recommend the use of such scholarship mobile apps as Scholarship.com, SAIL, Scholly, etc. Mobile apps, in many regards, work similarly to automatic alerts. A clear plus of resorting to scholarship mobile apps is that the most popular ones include scholarship statement summaries and built-in reminders and milestones. Two major downsides however are:

- Too many mobile apps are still poorly designed to track international scholarships even though they are rapidly improving.
- Using scholarship mobile apps might give the overall false impression that successfully applying for a scholarship is an easy click-through process. It might also keep students from actually going through the less appealing but yet comprehensive set of steps recommended throughout this guide. For example, by not always displaying or redirecting students to the original scholarship provider's website, some mobile apps do not give a full view or show all of the nuances of scholarship requirements. No mobile apps can replace the necessary effort and in-depth preparation required for success.
- At this time, I am personally still not convinced of the effectiveness of mobile apps when it comes to international scholarships application but I want to remain open-minded and optimistic for the near future and in this current fast-evolving technological environment.

DON'T FALL FOR THIS!!! HOW TO AVOID SCHOLARSHIP SCAMS

Worldwide, many unscrupulous people prey on students by setting up simple or sometimes elaborate schemes. The following are the most likely scams and financial fraud schemes you MUST be aware of and guard against!

- PAY TO PLAY SCHEMES: where you have to pay even the smallest amount.
- REFRAIN FROM PAYING ANYTHING TO A THIRD PARTY to either access scholarship information or for your scholarship application to be received or processed.
- REMEMBER THAT SCHOLARSHIP INFORMATION IS ALWAYS FREE and readily available online (original sources or reputable secondary sources) and at embassies, cultural centers, multilateral organizations, etc.
- DO NOT PAY! EVEN WHEN YOU ARE PROMISED TO GET YOUR MONEY BACK in case you are not successful. Experience shows that your chances of getting part or all of your money back are very very slim.
- SCHOLARSHIP LOTTERY OR AWAITING SCHOLARSHIPS: never pay to enter any supposed scholarship lotteries or to be signed up on supposed scholarship waiting lists. Never give in to calls to "claim your scholarship today!"
- SO-CALLED SCHOLARSHIP SERVICES offering to apply on your behalf. Do it yourself! Apply using the method described in this book and take charge of your application. Apply for every single scholarship yourself.
- PAY-FOR-LOAN schemes or PAY A LITTLE FEE IN ORDER TO RECEIVE AN AFFORDABLE LOAN. Student are required to pay an apparently insignificant fee upfront in exchange for an education loan. Be wary of having to pay for anything, even if you are promised affordable education loans or tuition discounts.
- "APPLY TODAY OR YOU WILL MISS A GREAT OPPORTUNITY" schemes. Some scammers pressure you to commit money and apply urgently. The only deadline that matters is the one on the provider's website.

35

- ALL YOU HAVE TO DO IS ENTER YOUR PERSONAL INFORMATION and you will receive a scholarship scheme. Never allow anyone to rush you into providing your personal information to a third party. Again, do it yourself! Apply the method described in this book and take charge of your application. Apply for every single scholarship yourself.
- PAY (BRIBE) SOMEONE IN "HIGH PLACES" so then can give you a scholarship. Never pay or trust any intermediaries. Stay away from and denounce corruption schemes.
- PAY FOR "DOUBIOUS" FINANCIAL ADVICE DISGUISED AS A "SCHOLARSHIP SEMINAR". Many unscrupulous salespersons posing as financial advisors may have you and your parents pay for scholarship "seminars" which are in reality sales platforms to promote financial/insurance services to you. Again, never pay for any financial advice supposedly designed to help you attain your scholarship goals. Run away from them as far as you can as they have nothing to do with scholarship advice.

REPORT ANY BRIBERY SOLICITATION, dubious scholarship-related activities, and fraud to the appropriate law enforcement authorities in your country. Do not waste your time and money on schemes which will not add any value to your scholarship quest.

There is no such thing as a hidden scholarship database that would be exclusively available to you through certain intermediaries.

ALWAYS:

- Do the research yourself
- When searching, start by looking into free local sources: your high school or college counselor, your local library
- Use free national sources: local representatives of foreign embassies, international cultural centers, regional cooperation, and multinational organizations, etc.
- Focus your search on original and free online sources: look at the scholarship provider's website thoroughly. Do not rush. Do it patiently!
- Search and apply from a large enough "pool" of scholarships. For example:

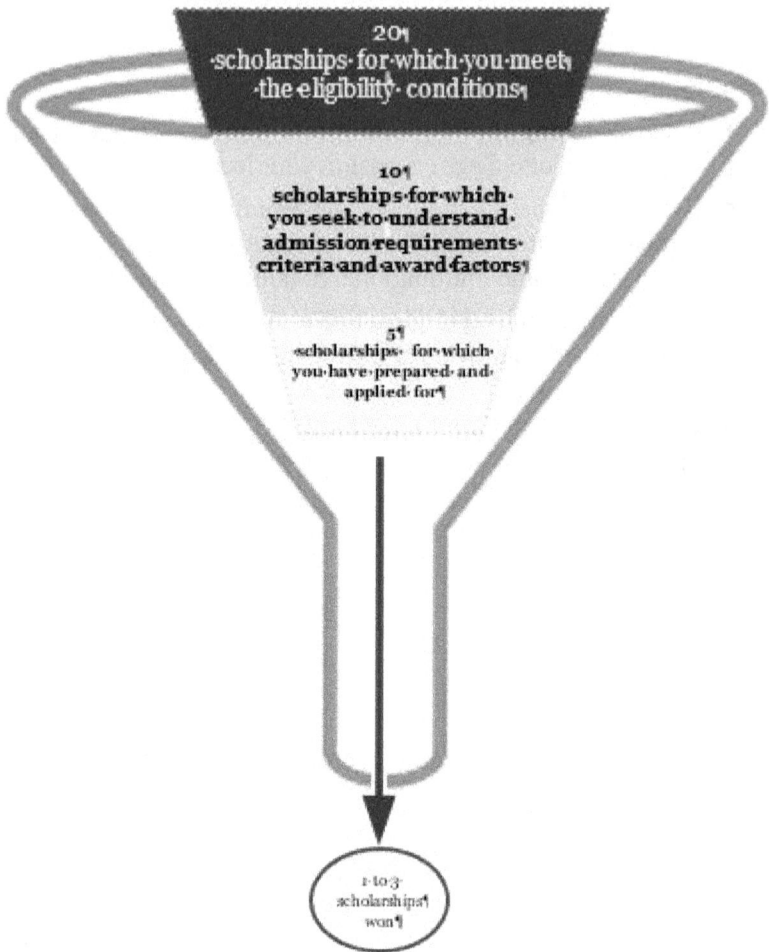

Fig 9: The scholarship funnel

THE BEST TOOLS IN YOUR SEARCH TOOLKIT

To all non-English speakers!
When doing an online search for scholarships, keep in mind that many websites, regardless of host country, are set up using key words in English. This is particularly true when it comes to international scholarships. It is strongly advised that you start by building a basic or advanced vocabulary of the most common

38

words used in international higher education for the country you are targeting.

Many scholarship landing pages are set up in a language which may not be English. Therefore, if your native language is not English, I recommend that you do some of your search relying on search engines with the extension of your country/language. For example, google.fr if you are in France or are a mostly French speaker. This move will improve your chances of yielding the most relevant results.

A FEW REPUTABLE SPECIALIZED WEBSITES

The internet is a fantastic tool which can give you access to virtually unlimited information, but not everything on the internet is relevant or true. In order to avoid getting swamped with inaccurate, blatantly false or irrelevant information, you are encouraged to resort to a few reputable specialized websites. Over the years, those websites have done a decent job at patiently compiling and organizing data about scholarship programs worldwide. Some have built a reputation for providing relative quality information and can be a source for basic information about scholarships. Although we do not endorse any of them and recommend that you be careful about hidden advertisement schemes used on some of those websites, they could be used as tools in your scholarship toolkit to help built a basic scholarship list:

- www.internationalstudent.com/scholarships
- https://bigfuture.collegeboard.org/scholarship-search
- www.idea-phd.net/index.php/en/funding-opportunities
- www.iefa.org/scholarships
- https://applications.wes.org/scholarship-finder/
- www.scholarshipportal.com
- www.scholars4dev.com
- http://www.cucas.edu.cn/china_scholarships
- www.opportunitiesforafricans.com
- https://www.studyinaustralia.gov.au/english/australian-education/scholarships/

THREE

Three
A goldmine hiding in plain sight A for Attention to details, A for Analysis

"Dedicate time to understanding the scholarship statement and beyond because any hastily put together application is bound to fail." Anonymous Educational Adviser

After reading this chapter, you should be able to:
- Understand the intricate differences between eligibility conditions, admission requirements, selection criteria, and key award factors
- Determine how and where to find out information about the key factors for a specific scholarship
- Understand how to use alumni insights to enhance your application

READING IN BETWEEN, BEHIND AND BEYOND THE LINES
A for Attention to details
IN YOUR SEARCH, YOU MAY COME ACROSS SUCH WORDS AS CRITERIA OR REQUIREMENTS. You could be tempted to underestimate their true meaning or be confused as to what is exactly expected of you. Strive to always deeply understand the scholarship application process and its nuances as that understanding is a very important asset that will save you a great deal of time and frustration further down the road.

One of the "secrets" to fine-tuning your scholarship application and making it stand out is the intricate understanding of the differences between the scholarship eligibility conditions, the

41

admission requirements set for the scholarship and/or the program you are applying for, the selection criteria, and the key award factors that make the scholarship judges "tick".

Picture a target with multiple successive concentric circles. The outer edge (annulus) is represented by the eligibility conditions. In the center are the key award factors, or the bullseye. In between the bullseye and the annulus are the selection criteria and admission requirements.

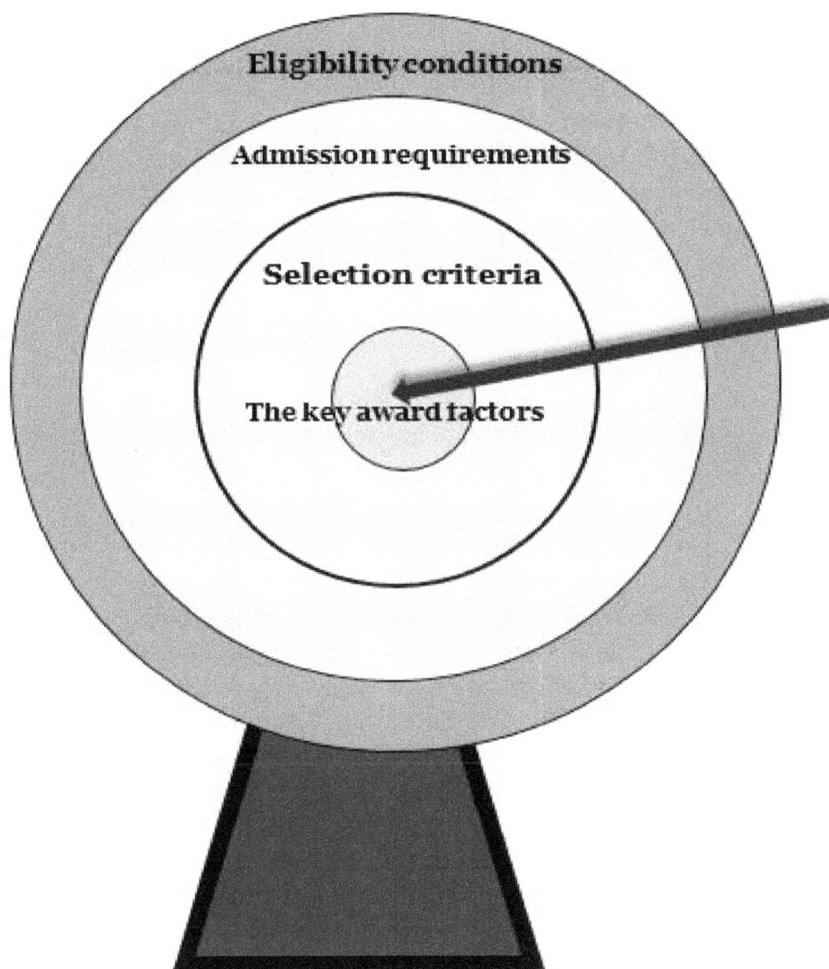

Fig 10: Understanding the importance of each level of scholarship criteria

Unfortunately, most applicants only put their efforts in aiming for the eligibility conditions and the admission requirements when they should also look to understand and meet the selection criteria and the key award factors

Your goal should be not just to hit the target anywhere within those concentric circles but to reach the center of it with precision. The next paragraphs show you how.

While the information on scholarship eligibility and admission criteria is pretty straight forward and easy to identify and understand, the selection criteria and the awards factors are often much more subtle and harder to decipher...Your ultimate goal is to reach the heart of the target by accurately meeting the award factors.

Eligibility conditions

Eligibility condition is a list of preconditions posted by the scholarship provider. Eligibility includes:

- Who can apply: maximum age limit, gender, citizenship or residency requirements, field of specialization, main areas of scholarship focus, the main (stated) objective of the scholarship;
- The process description and deadlines: key deadlines, process time line, and application review and, interview dates.

Eligibility conditions take the form of a one or two paragraph summary. They should state the smallest common denominator among all would-be applicants; the "lowest bar" to meet in order to get an application started. It provides the basic information about the scholarship and sometimes specifies if the scholarship is merit and/or need based. You are strongly encouraged to read beyond the eligibility conditions. For example, the prestigious L'Oréal-Unesco fellowship solely targets women in the sciences who are citizens or residents of countries in Africa, the Middle East, North and South America, Europe and Asia Pacific. Obviously, if you are neither a woman nor from the targeted world regions, there is no need for you to apply.

The admission requirements

These are the complete list of required paperwork, minimum degree requirements, official degrees and transcripts, customized or standardized academic, content or language skills tests (GMAT, Toefl, TAGE MAGE, etc.), essays (format and prompts), recommendation or reference letters to submit, the submission format and, the possible exemptions. The requirements also include the terms of the scholarship: how much funding is made available, what is covered and is not and for how long. Sometimes the admission requirements state the maximum number of awards per year or per cycle.

It is estimated that up to 90% of applicants are eliminated just through the very first application review process. Therefore, eligibility conditions and admission requirements are important and should be carefully met even though they only represent a small fraction of a successful scholarship application.

While the first two sets of criteria (eligibility conditions and admission requirements) are routinely discussed in the "scholarship literature", the following two (selection criteria and award factors) are usually glanced over or ignored despite the crucial edge they give to successful scholarship applications.

Selection criteria

These are criteria which do not necessarily show on eligibility or admission requirements. They are nevertheless just as (if not more) important when building a robust application. They are usually implied in the eligibility and admission requirements, they are sometimes spelled out and refer to the underlying philosophy of a given scholarship program. As an applicant, you should strive to find out what type of students a scholarship program is really (really) looking to fund. You should be able to read in-between the lines of stated eligibility and admission criteria and spot the unspoken criteria.

In other words, you should be able to find the criteria behind the criteria by looking for the information on the scholarship program or provider's original website. Make sure to always get your information from the original scholarship program's we bite or promotional documents. One way to achieve that goal is to thoroughly read the "About us" section on the scholarship provider's website. Selection criteria also answer the following question:

- What is really going to make my application stand out beyond just meeting eligibility and admission requirements?

- How can I smartly interpret the stated scholarship program's mission and goals?
- How competitive is the selection and award process?

All the information gathered must be used to fine tune your application and give it more depth. The information could, for example, help improve the way you go about requesting or drafting your recommendation letters.

The key award factors

This step is about getting to understand in very fine terms how the final selection and scholarship award is done. This step is usually the best kept secret. It is still very mysterious. What are, among all the selection criteria, the ones that are truly going to give your application a definite edge and make a difference? Why should I receive the award instead of somebody else? Our section about attention to detail explains where and how to find information about such unwritten criteria as the critical importance of grammatically spotless essays for many judges, or current trends in applicant profile. You should inquire about the relative weight of those key factors in the application. You must also try to find out what is discussed during the judging of scholarship applications for the scholarship you are applying for. Objectively determine what your strengths and weaknesses are with regards to the admission and selection criteria. Again, use the information you would have garnered to your advantage to continually strengthen your application.

SCHOLARSHIP WINNERS TIPS!
AN EXAMPLE OF UNWRITTEN CRITERIA: TYPOS AND GRAMMATICAL ERRORS
Although typos and grammatical errors are not usually viewed as scholarship criteria, they can be just as detrimental to any application as applying a very low GPA. Sometimes, scholarship providers or judges have a very low tolerance for typos and other similar errors. Not carefully proofreading your work can prove fatal. It is said that up to 10% of international scholarship applications are eliminated by scholarship processing committees in the first review because one of their goals is to

46

reduce the number of qualifying applicants to "humanely manageable" proportions. This step is necessary before scholarship processing committees can start delving into the pool of applicants who meet the eligibility and admission criteria discussed in earlier chapters. They would use any excuse to reduce their workload. That is fair game. The truth is, your application will be "tossed out" in the first round of review for such reasons as untidiness, incompleteness, spelling errors, missing supporting documents, late test score submission, missed or blank fields or incomplete answers, just to name a few. This sorting out process is sometimes called the winnowing process. It is meant to quickly get rid of applications which may contain apparent or obvious flaws and to only keep the ones deemed worthy of a second or third review... and eventually of an award.

Do not allow small errors or the lack of detailed attention ruin the hard work you put into drafting the "ideal" essay or putting together letters of recommendation, preparing, and taking the required tests, etc.

During the information gathering phase, you must continue to stay organized and methodical.

SECRETS THAT SHOULD NOT BE KEPT SECRET

A for Analysis: Using alumni testimonials and advice, online discussion forums to your advantage

Alumni testimonials and advice

Look for recent testimonials (online or in print) made by people who have received the targeted scholarship in the past. Try to attend gatherings where they meet, approach associations they belong to, read their memos and take careful note of the public comments they make. Ask each alumnus you get a chance to interact with this important question: "what are the 3 to 5 factors that made you successful in winning this scholarship?" Don't be shy. Write their response down and get immediately to work implementing their advice. Do not waste time!

Online discussion forums
Look for reputable online discussion forums where past or prospective candidates meet and exchange views and tips. Read the questions and answers provided on forums and ask relevant questions, but take the information provided with a grain of salt. Try as much as possible to corroborate this information with what is available on official school and scholarship providers' websites as well as on promotional documentation. If you patiently and methodically follow, the afore-mentioned two pieces of advice, this will prove to be a real asset.

A NOTE ABOUT STUDY ABROAD PROGRAMS

Study abroad programs are usually educational programs run via a university and whereby students spend a semester or two (sometimes longer) at a university outside of their country of residence.
The excitement of attending a study abroad program is almost always damped by the cost of most of them. It is a little-known secret that there are multiple scholarships available worldwide even for study abroad programs.

Study abroad can be:

- Merit-based (Read Part 2)
- Need-based (Read Part 2)
- Destination-specific. Whereby foreign governments or institutions might offer scholarships as an incentive to encourage students from other countries to pursue schooling or research in their country.
- Subject-specific. Whereby monetary awards are made available mainly based on the applicant's field of study or research.
- A combination of all of the above categories of scholarships.

Here again, success in securing funding rests upon following the careful steps offered throughout this book.

FOUR

FOUR
Rising up to the occasion P for Preparation, P for Perseverance

"By failing to prepare, you are preparing to fail."
Benjamin Franklin

After reading this chapter, you should be able to:
- Assess your strengths and weaknesses with regards to the scholarship requirements and criteria
- Draft great essays, personal statements and, study objectives
- Understand the importance of recommendation letters
- Help draft outstanding recommendation letters on your behalf
- Know how to go about credential submission

Moving from average to good: P for Preparation
Once you have a solid understanding of both the explicit and the implied criteria and of all of their nuances, you can start planning and preparing for your application. Using the updated scholarship summary (Read Part 2), determine how you currently measure up against every single criterion today. The following proven and powerful analytical approach is borrowed from the business consulting world. What are your strengths and weaknesses as well as the external opportunities and threats that may impact your preparation and which cannot be underestimated? Adjust your scholarship preparation and application plans accordingly. Many scholarship recipients have wisely decided to delay their application by a year after

acknowledging that one of their key weaknesses had to be fixed or remedied before they could apply.

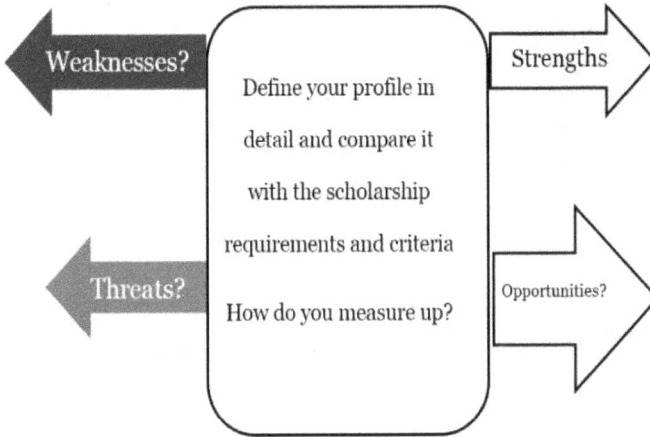

Weaknesses? Strengths

Define your profile in

detail and compare it

with the scholarship

requirements and criteria

Threats? Opportunities?

How do you measure up?

Fig 11: prospective applicant's strengths, weaknesses, threats, and opportunities assessments

Strengths: evaluate what your strengths (personal, professional, academic, leadership, etc.) are with regards to the scholarship requirements and criteria

Weaknesses: evaluate what your weaknesses are with regards to the scholarship requirements and criteria.

Opportunities: list what in your current work, study or social environment can constitute an opportunity you can capitalize on when preparing your application

Threats: list what in your current work, study or social environment could potentially slow down or halt your progress

Weakness: I was not top of my class

Define your profile in detail and compare it with the scholarship requirements and criteria

How do you measure up?

Strength: I have been a very involved youth leader in the last 3 years

Threat: no particular external threats

Opportunity: recent alumni have shown strong leadership potential

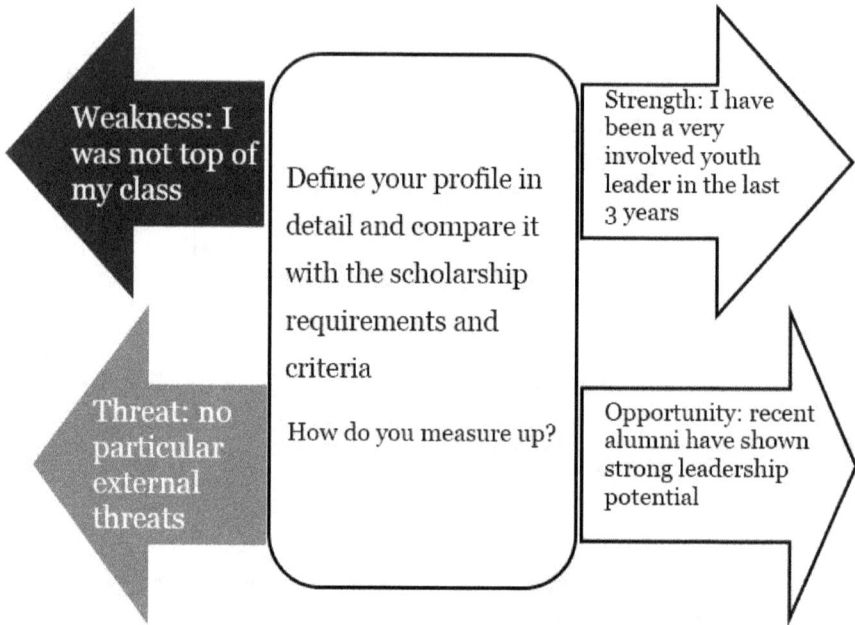

Fig 12: applied strengths, weaknesses, threats, and opportunities assessments

To prepare is to work hard and smartly over a period of time in order to bridge not just any gaps, but the ones you identified as you compared yourself to the criteria. To prepare is really to work to meet and exceed each criterion individually as much as possible... Get to work!!!

Take the time to prepare thoroughly on every single item.

How to write great essays

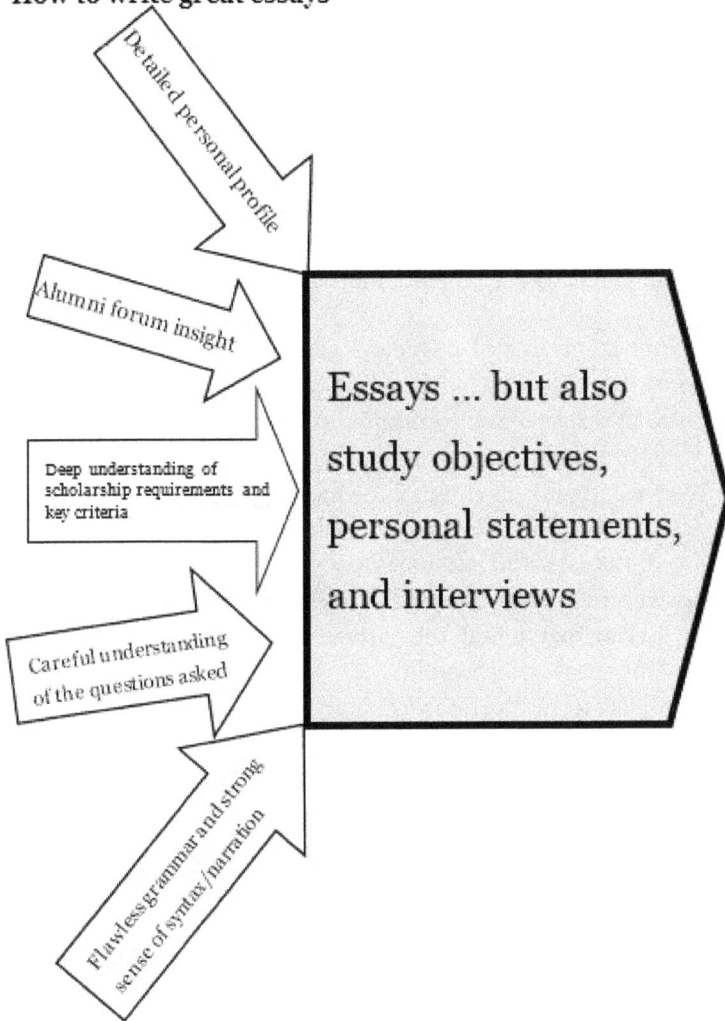

Detailed personal profile

Alumni forum insight

Deep understanding of scholarship requirements and key criteria

Essays ... but also study objectives, personal statements, and interviews

Careful understanding of the questions asked

Flawless grammar and strong sense of syntax/narration

Fig 13: indispensable ingredients to a great essay

Let me be clear, essays are one of the most important parts of your application regardless of your strengths on other aspects of your application, namely GPA, grades, test scores, etc. Take the necessary time to work on drafting your essay. Never rush through it. Fortunately, if you have described your profile as prescribed in chapter 2 of this book and have sought to deeply understand the selection criteria and award factors, drafting your essay will be a smooth ride. Since you will not have the opportunity to personally meet with the members of scholarship award committees to introduce yourself, shake hands and explain why you, amongst thousands of applicants, deserve to receive the scholarship, essays are the only way for you to do just that. It is your way of giving scholarship judges an accurate portrayal of who you are, of your potential (academic, leadership, etc.), your passion, motivations, and future goals.

15 Characteristics of a Great Essay
A great essay must:
- Show to the selection committee why you should be granted the scholarship
- Weave and glue together all the moving "parts" of your application package (past achievements, test scores, interests, and passion, etc.)
- Answer the questions asked or address the prompt all while tying together all the parts of the application. Do not unnecessarily ramble.
- Display your motivations for applying in the first place.
- Display your achievements. Do not be shy about them. Do not brag about them either.
- Inspire the reader by displaying your leadership, endurance, mental strengths, or social and community service... Do not exaggerate.
- Have an introduction, a body, and a conclusion. Make sure your introduction is grabbing and energetic. Make sure your body flows and is easy to read. Make sure your conclusion is not just a summary but leaves the reader with food for thought.
- Rely upon your deep knowledge of the selection criteria, and award factors (Read again Part 3) and display how your application relates to those two sets of criteria.
- Clearly display your career goals and future professional plans. What difference would it make to your life, to the provider, to the world...

- Display why you are a good fit for the program and possibly what you could bring to the table to help fulfill the scholarship provider's missions
- Be unique and describe your distinctive narrative, give your personal angle, shed light on relevant parts of your life.
- Not contain any plagiarism. Avoid using original essays from other people or readily available online templates.
- Meticulously be proofread for spelling, grammar, and syntax error. Have it reviewed repeatedly by friends, family, past scholarship winners etc.
- Contain illustrative examples. Don't just state broad principles, say how they may apply to you.
- Display how you overcame challenges or what was the turning point in your life, if any.

Also, feel free to read such a great book as *How To Write a Winning Scholarship* Essay by Gen and Kelly Tanabe.

Note on study objectives and personal statements
In many graduate level scholarship applications, you may be asked to submit, in addition or instead of your essay, a study objective and/or a personal statement. The prompts are typically straight-forward. Make sure to directly respond to questions asked. This may go without saying but make sure the essay rules about having a clear introduction-body-conclusion and extensive proofreading are also followed.

Tips for outstanding scholarship interviews
In some cases, you will be required to take an interview over the phone, through videoconferencing or face-to-face. Here again, a clear and detailed outline of your own profile as well as a solid understanding of the apparent and hidden criteria should provide you with the material for your responses.
- Choose a quiet and adequately lit setting.
- Draw on your profile outline.
- Listen very carefully to the interviewer's questions.
- Take written notes.

- Feel free to ask the interviewer to repeat their questions if need be
- Answer the questions precisely.
- Make sure to draw on your understanding of what types of applicants the judges are looking for.
- Speak loud enough in your most intelligible voice.
- Don't use jargon and complicated wording or explanation.
- Feel free to take a few seconds to gather your thoughts if need be.
- Before the interview, write some expected questions and some of your possible responses.

Preparing for required standardized tests and for learning a new language

Standardized tests are a key component of scholarship applications. The most common standardized tests required for the sake of not just college/university admission, but also scholarship application, are SAT, GMAT, TAGE MAGE, and Toefl. Many scholarship committee members admit that during the first or even second selection round, they would pick applicants with the highest standardized scores first. It is apparently much easier and less time-consuming to sort out applicants based on a "number", namely standardized scores. Faced with limited human resource, scholarship judges would look at "score numbers" instead of having to read through long application packages. That is understandable. You should therefore never neglect standardized test preparation. Take the time to self-prepare and/or hire a coach/instructor if necessary. The extra effort will be well worth it. It is not uncommon for the scholarship winner to devote several months in order to prepare for such standardized tests as the GRE or TOEFL, even if that would mean delaying your application by a year or more.

How to (smartly) request for (strong) recommendation letters

Recommendation letters, just like essays, give scholarship judges a glimpse of who you really are. Unlike essays, which are direct narratives coming from you, recommendations letters are narratives/assessments coming from third parties, through their eyes. Therefore, take them very seriously.

- Regardless of how many letters of recommendation your application demands, list 2 to 4 additional potential recommender's, as the initial people you go to might not respond. Avoid people who used to report to you and avoid family members.
- Make sure to ask potential recommenders if they would be able to provide a good or a great recommendation for you
- Start months ahead of time!!! Never by the deadline.
- Make sure you request a diverse group of people who know you and who can speak to each facet or area of your career/life and personality (academic, professional, extracurricular).
- Always ask for their full names, preferably professional email and/or postal addresses, exact past, and current titles.
- Ask if you could send them an outline of what you would like to be included in the letter of recommendation. This step can help speed up the process of drafting and submitting the recommendation letter. It can also refine the content of the letter. Even though you are not supposed to know what is in a recommendation letter submitted on your behalf, this step allows you to "guess" what could be said about you.
- Make sure to suggest outlines that differ from one recommender to another. Ideally, be sure to have different aspects and angles of your career, life, and schooling, emphasized in each outline.
- Double check with the scholarship providing institution to see if all letters of recommendation have been submitted as promised by your recommenders.

Submitting your transcripts and other credentials

- Give instruction for sending your transcripts and diplomas from your alma mater or the relevant institution directly to the scholarship provider very early on.
- Request translation and third-party evaluation services whenever applicable.
- Always make sure to have a detailed subject and credit hour description sheet sent along with your transcripts as institutions outside of your country may not always understand or know how to interpret the content of your transcripts and credentials. Don't assume they do.

MOVING FROM GOOD TO GREAT: P FOR PERSEVERANCE

"When obstacles arise, you change your direction to reach your goal; you do not change your initial decision to get there." Zig Ziglar

Example of criteria	You today	What still needs to be done
Required minimum English iBT Toefl score of 110	Toefl score of 97	Self-prepare and/or enroll in a Toefl prep program
3 letters of recommendations	You don't have any idea where to start	• → Reach out to 4 to 6 potential strong recommenders • → Clearly explain what is expected • → Offer to draft a letter or an outline in order to get the process started (Part 2, section 1)

Fig 14: assessing your progress| Turning weaknesses into strengths

MOVING FROM (GREAT) POTENTIAL TO (GREAT) DELIVERY

BAD NEWS! Applying for a scholarship is rarely an easy ride. As you journey through the preparation phase, you will undoubtedly go through times when you may feel discouraged or powerless when faced with growing amount of work or when a higher degree of focus is demanded of you. Especially, if you have to keep juggling other priorities of your life at the same time: family, work, school, extracurricular activities.

Most common reasons scholarship applicants may give up:
- Not getting a "high enough" test score despite your continuous preparation.
- Feeling of not being able to improve your essay draft.

- Feeling overwhelmed by the amount of preparative work required to draft a sound study or research objective statement.
- Not being able to get top recommendation letters drafted on your behalf and within the deadline.
- Poor or low foreign language skills.
- Missed deadlines.

GOOD NEWS! Your steadfastness in preparing and perfecting your application regardless of bumps in the road, and your unshakable tenacity and determination are key qualities you can cultivate and use.

Many scholarship applicants use the following techniques to help them stay focused and mentally strong:

- Accountability partner: share your preparation goals with a close or trusted friend, family member or a scholarship alumnus AND ask them to keep checking your progress with you and motivate you as needed.

- Taking full advantage of electronic calendars, deadline reminders and milestone alerts to keep track of your progress.

- Making time to relax and get your mind busy somewhere else while you take a break from your scholarship application preparation.

FIVE

FIVE

It's not over until it's over E for Execution, E for Evaluation

"There is a deep sea between saying and doing." Italian proverb

After reading this chapter, you should be able to:
- Learn how to stay focused throughout the application process
- Learn what to do once you have been notified you won a scholarship
- Learn how to plan for the long term and how to fully benefit from your international experience

Flawless execution: E for Execution

Execution refers to following through on your commitment to turning your weakest points into strong ones within the time frame set. More importantly, making sure to plan to gather all of the documents and submit or have submitted everything required directly to the scholarship provider way ahead of the deadline.

Flawless execution is being able to accurately coordinate and time multiple preparation tracks (i.e. test preparation, profile strengthening, essay writing, letters of recommendation drafting etc.). It is critically important.

All throughout the search and preparation process, keep a close eye on your calendar (Read Part 1). Most importantly incorporate each submission deadlines in your planning and set specific milestones completion dates accordingly. Adjust those completion date as necessary and as you progress. Be flexible, but make sure to allow yourself enough time cushion for completion of your milestones. Many experts recommend that every required application item should be reviewed using a checklist and turned in at least 12 to 14 weeks before the official deadline.

Submit your application early: many scholarship programs operate on a "first come, first served" basis. The scholarship judges review applications as they arrive before the selection committee. Submitting your application package way ahead of time gives you some cushion in case an item or a document is missing or delayed for reasons beyond your control.

Always make sure you request or receive an acknowledgment of receipt either electronically, on paper, or verbally depending on whether your application is in electronic or paper format. Do the same for every single scholarship you apply for.
An increasing number of scholarships requires an electronic application. Make sure you log onto the scholarship application interface, create an account and thoroughly populate it: provide as much information and details as you possibly can. Never leave any application questions unanswered, even the ones for which you may not have immediate articulate answers. Take the time to ponder each question including those which at first glance might sound easy or self-evident; carefully draft each answer and have it reviewed and proofread by a third party.

If you have selected more than one scholarship and are planning to apply for each of them consecutively therefore, prepare and apply for the ones with the earliest deadlines first. In addition to closely keeping track of application deadlines, monitor scholarship or award notification dates so you can verify when the names of the winners are announced. Start by checking the scholarship with the earliest notification date and go on to the next earliest one.

E for Evaluation: am I on the right track?

You have submitted your application package, what's next?

Many applicants wonder what to do once they have submitted their application. Following is a list of questions and answers to help you make sense of the immediate post-submission period:

Can I check on the status of my application?
You should go by what is recommended by each scholarship you have applied for. Many scholarship programs specifically discourage applicants to email or call to check on the status of applications. Verify that is the case in your particular situation and strictly adhere to the requirement. Do NOT reach out them! An increasing number of scholarship programs provide online status update and/or an award announcement date. Here again, patiently wait for them to reach out to you. Typically, only winners are notified. If you have not been contacted by the scholarship committee by the stated award date, chances are you did not win.
If you are unclear about any restrictions, email a scholarship admission officer once: be very concise and inquire about the status of your applications.

What is the award announcement date?
It is the date stated by the scholarship providers or by the organization that manages the scholarship program on their behalf. It is usually clearly stated in the scholarship application package or on the scholarship provider's website.

What is a contingency plan? How do I create one?
A contingency plan is an objective and detailed list of actions you anticipate taking or a schedule of what you will be doing after you are notified of your award or after you realize you did not win. Evidently, the course of actions drastically differs from one outcome to another. Contingency plans must therefore clearly address the following questions: "what do I need to do, now that I won" or adversely "what do I need to do now that I did not win".

64

By helping you think through the scholarship notification aftermath, drafting a contingency plan, can also help you remove or reduce the level of anxiety usually associated with post-scholarship notification. It triggers further reflections and actions such as: can you imagine your academic and professional career without the scholarship? How does the scholarship going to affect other compartments of my life (family, finance, social, intellectual etc.)? How to (re)evaluate your needs? How to practically get ready for departure?

What is the first thing to do as soon as I receive my scholarship award notification?
Once you are formally notified by the provider that you won a scholarship, the very first thing to do is to decide whether to accept, postponed or reject the award.

In rare occasions, you may consider postponing or rejecting the offer for which you have been working so hard. Your decision should always be based on a thorough assessment of every potential adverse factors (family emergency, better scholarship, or professional offers, unresolved significant financial constraints etc.) never on perception.

Make whoever notified you know of your decision within a couple of days. Always thank them and show gratitude.

How are scholarship award typically announced?
Scholarships are usually announced directly by the provider or the managing organization via official electronic or more commonly regular mail, rarely via phone calls. Announcements are almost always made in plain language. They include the conditions and restrictions of the award as well as the option to either accept or refuse them.

Now what? What is a "post-decision" checklist?
It is the list of actions to take after you are formally notified you won a scholarship.

That checklist includes:
- **A formal acknowledgement of receipt** of the award and the acceptance or rejection of the award

65

- **Detailed material and financial assessment**. You are encouraged to objectively evaluate how the scholarship award is going to impact your current material and financial life and plan accordingly. For example, if you are still receiving wages from an employer or are also the recipient of another scholarship, the scholarship provider may decide to lower or adjust their award.

- **Detailed social, academic, and/or professional assessment**. You are also encouraged to objectively anticipate how the award is going to affect your current family, school, or work arrangements throughout the time of your program overseas and plan/adjust accordingly. For example, you may consider taking a prolonged leave of absence from work or plan to relocate with your immediate family even if those decisions may be financially costly.

- **Detailed immediate and day-by-day preparation** at least 6 months prior to your academic start date. More practically, you are encouraged to make sure you are ready when it comes to such items as: preparation for the travel (visa, airfare ticket, complete physicals; vaccination, and immunizations, etc.), preparation for your new academic and social life (reach out to the international student or scholar office at your future host institution for further information). Start connecting with people and organizations that you might be of interest to you in the host country. Continue to improve your knowledge of the language and culture of the host country/community even after you are notified of a scholarship award. Continue to maintain good grades. Make several copies of your important documents and keep one set in your home country.

- **Detailed post-scholarship program goals and timeline**. Start planning what you anticipate getting out of your international scholarship opportunity. Start thinking about where you want to be academically/professionally and what you want to do as soon as you are notified of your scholarship award.

How should I handle a negative response?

If you learn that you did not receive the scholarship you applied for, do not be discouraged. Most international scholarships are very competitive. The outcome is therefore not necessarily a reflection on your value or your hard work. You may consider reapplying for the same scholarship later or for other ones. Before doing so, make sure to methodically use any feedback you can gather after your rejection to strengthen your future applications.

Enjoying and benefiting from your experience overseas

While your degree or research program is ongoing, make sure to participate or be active in academic, professional, and social networking organizations. When your program is winding down, join existing or start a network of alumni beneficiaries/awardees. Always strive to live up to the ideals that lead you to apply for an international scholarship in the first place. Remember, scholarships exist for a reason. Pass on the torch! Be a mentor to would-be college or scholarship applicants! Be a mentor or an advisor to students and scholars! Inspire the youth! Inspire others!

FINAL
THOUGHTS

FINAL THOUGHTS

In reality, there is no such thing as a secret to winning international scholarships. The selection of tips and the best practices wrapped in the mental attitudes and indomitable work ethic promoted throughout the chapters of this guide are only meant as tools to help you in your scholarship quest. It is now up to you to use tools and apply them for success. This book, by no means, completes our lifelong exploration of the fascinating subject of international scholarships. It is a work in progress. We are committed to continuing enriching its content. In the coming years, we will be incorporating feedback and new tips from students, scholarship providers and, higher education professionals worldwide.

RECOMMENDED READINGS (AND OTHERS GOOD RESOURCES)

Recommended readings

- Filip, Ruxandra. (2016). MEXT Scholarship 2016-2017 (Research, Master, PhD): Your complete eBook guide to applying for the Monbukagakusho Research Scholarship in Japan (My Japanese Experience). Kindle Edition.
- Gamontle, Bojosi (2014). Scholarships for Africans: A guide to successfully applying for admission and funding for Masters and Ph.D. degrees. Kindle Edition.
- Tanabe, Kelly and Tanabe, Gen (2014). How to Write a Winning Scholarship Essay: 30 Essays That Won Over $3 Million in Scholarships. Super College, Belmont, California, USA.

Good resources

IELTS: International English Language Testing System is an international standardized test of English language proficiency for non-native English language speakers. www.ielts.org/en-us

GMAT: Graduate Management Admission Test. Test intended to assess certain analytical, writing, quantitative, verbal, and reading skills in written English for use in admission to such graduate management programs as MBA's. www.mba.com

HSK (the Chinese Proficiency Test): an international standardized test of Chinese language proficiency which assesses non-native Chinese speakers' abilities in using the Chinese language. www.chinesetest.cn/gosign.do?lid=0

TAGE MAGE: Test d'Aptitude aux études de Gestion et au Management des Entreprises. Assesses analytical, writing, quantitative, verbal, and reading skills in written French for use in admission to graduate management programs.www.tagemage.fr

Super College: great college admission tips www.supercollege.com

APPENDIXES

APPENDIX#1
International scholarship checklist

APPENDIX#2
Sample list of attributes in nationally competitive scholarships

APPENDIX#3
Examples of scholarships per host country/world region or per student's country of origin

APPENDIX#4
Good source for worldwide grade correspondence

Appendix 1: international scholarship checklist

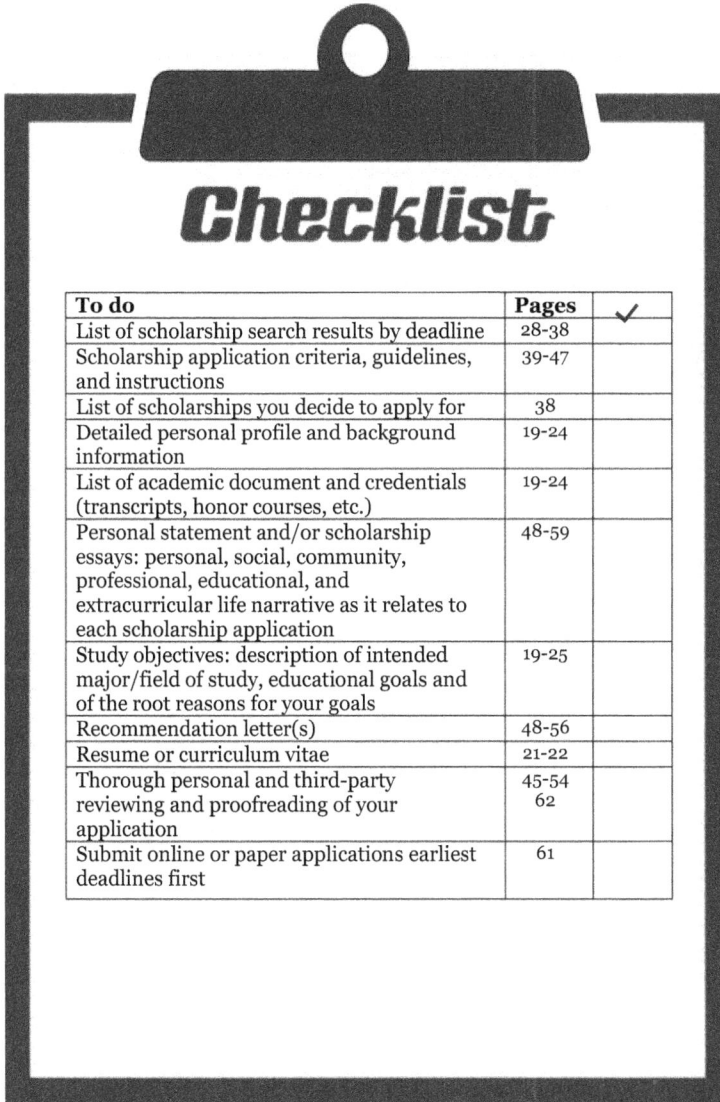

Checklist

To do	Pages	✓
List of scholarship search results by deadline	28-38	
Scholarship application criteria, guidelines, and instructions	39-47	
List of scholarships you decide to apply for	38	
Detailed personal profile and background information	19-24	
List of academic document and credentials (transcripts, honor courses, etc.)	19-24	
Personal statement and/or scholarship essays: personal, social, community, professional, educational, and extracurricular life narrative as it relates to each scholarship application	48-59	
Study objectives: description of intended major/field of study, educational goals and of the root reasons for your goals	19-25	
Recommendation letter(s)	48-56	
Resume or curriculum vitae	21-22	
Thorough personal and third-party reviewing and proofreading of your application	45-54 62	
Submit online or paper applications earliest deadlines first	61	

Appendix 2: key attributes scholarship providers look for in applications.

Sought-after attributes	✓
Ability to contribute to your field of study	
Activity in support of human rights, the rule of law and citizenry	
Adaptability	
Advancing the responsibilities of citizenship in free society	
Appreciation of participation in arts and humanities	
Leadership and capacity for future influence	
Clearly defined career interest	
Commitment to improving the commonwealth	
Commitment to integrating research and education	
Commitment to values in the U.S. Constitution and the Bill of Rights	
Communication skills	
Character, creative ability and, originality	
Critical-thinking ability	
Ethical character and integrity	
Experience in community service or development	
Initiative and leadership	
Intellectual distinction and merit	
Intelligence	
Intention to serve or current service in communities or countries of origin	
Interest in fellow human beings and for problems of society	
Personal promise of creative achievement and originality	
Potential for decision making	
Potential innovative research	
Potential for future achievement	
Potential to influence opinions	
Public service	
Respect for fellow human beings	
Scholarship	
Scholastic achievement	
Significant achievement	
Understanding of physical principles	
Vision	
Volunteerism	
Wide interests	

Adapted from Ilchman, Warren F., Ilchman, Alice S and, Tolar, Mary H. (2004). *The Lucky Few and the Worthy Many: Scholarship Competitions and the World's Future Leaders.* Philanthropic and Nonprofit Studies. Page 32 Table 2.1

Appendix 3: examples of scholarships per host country/world regions

EAP: East Asia and Pacific: scholarships for programs in East Asia and Pacific or for students from East Asia and Pacific
EE: Europe and Eurasia: scholarships for programs in Europe and Eurasia or for students from Europe and Eurasia
MENA: Middle East and North Africa: scholarships for programs in Middle East and North Africa or for students from Middle East and North Africa
SCA: South and Central Asia: scholarships for programs in South and Central Asia or for students from South and Central Asia
SSA: Sub-Saharan Africa: scholarships for programs in Sub-Saharan Africa or for students from Sub-Saharan Africa
WH: Western Hemisphere: Scholarships for programs in the Western Hemisphere (North, Central, South America and the Caribbean)

Scholarship programs or providing/host organizations	World regions
2017 Future Global Leaders Fellowship-Future Leaders Foundation www.futureleaders.org/about-the-fellowship	EAP|EE|MENA|SCA|SSA|WH
3ie Scholarship for International Development at the University of East Anglia www.3ieimpact.org/en/funding	EE
AAUW International Fellowships www.aauw.org/what-we-do/educational-funding-and-awards	EAP|EE|MENA|SCA|SSA|WH
Académie de Recherche et d'Enseignement supérieur (ARES) http://www.ares-ac.be/fr/bourses-csi	EAP|EE|MENA
ACLS Fellowships in Humanities for Africans: www.acls.org/programs/ahp	MENA
ACTFL American Council on the teaching of foreign language https://www.actfl.org/assessment-professional-development/scholarships-and-grants	EAP|EE|MENA|SCA|SSA|WH
ADB Scholarships at University of Auckland (New Zealand) https://www.auckland.ac.nz/en/study/international-students.html	EAP|MENA|SCA|SSA
ADB-Japan Scholarship Program for Developing Countries in Asia and Pacific www.adb.org/site/careers/japan-scholarship-program/main	EAP|SCA
Adelaide International Undergraduate Scholarships (AIUS) https://international.adelaide.edu.au/choosing/scholarships/aius	EAP| MENA|SCA|SSA
African Development Bank Young Professionals Program www.afdb.org/en/about-us/careers/young-professionals-program-ypp	EAP|EE|MENA|SCA|SSA|WH
African Leadership in Business MBA Scholarships-ALB Foundation www.albfoundation.org/about-mba-scholarships	MENA|SSA
African Union (AU) Scholarships- Pan African University www.pau-au.net	MENA|SSA

Scholarship programs or providing/host organizations (continued)	World regions
Aga Khan Foundation International Scholarship Program www.akdn.org/our-agencies/aga-khan-foundation/international-scholarship-programme	EAP|MENA|SCA|SSA
Alexander Graham Bell Association for the Deaf and Hard of Hearing https://www.agbell.org/Document.aspx?id=266	EAP|EE|MENA|SCA|SSA|WH
Allan & Nesta Ferguson Charitable Trust Masters Scholarships at University of Sheffield	EAP|EE|MENA|SCA|SSA|WH
Albright Institute Fellowships: www.wellesley.edu/albright/fellowship/fellows	EAP|EE|MENA|SCA|SSA|WH
Alexander Graham Bell Association for the Deaf and Hard of Hearing https://www.agbell.org/Document.aspx?id=266	EAP|EE|MENA|SCA|SSA|WH
Allan & Nesta Ferguson Charitable Trust Masters Scholarships at University of Sheffield www.sheffield.ac.uk/international/money/fergusonscholarship	EAP|EE|MENA|SCA|SSA|WH
Allen Lee Hughes Fellowship: www.arena-stage.org/about/employment/fellow_info.shtml	SSA
Alma Graduate School Africa MBA Scholarship Program www.gsb.stanford.edu/programs/mba/financial-aid/international-students	EAP|EE|MENA|SCA|SSA|WH
American Nuclear Society (ANS) Graduate Scholarships: http://ans.org/honors/scholarships/	EE|WH
American Scandinavian Foundation http: www.amscan.org/fellowship.html	EAP|EE|MENA|SCA|SSA|WH
American University Emerging Global Leader Scholarship: www.american.edu/admissions/international/egls.cfm	EAP|EE|MENA|SCA|SSA|WH
Amherst College Scholarships: www.amherst.edu/offices/financialaid/international_students/financialaid_award	EAP|EE|MENA|SCA|SSA|WH
Ampère Excellence Scholarships for International Students: www.ens-lyon.fr/en/grants-and-scholarships-279258.kjsp	EAP|EE|MENA|SCA|SSA|WH
Amsterdam Excellence Scholarships -AES (Netherlands): www.uva.nl/en/education/master-s/scholarships--tuition/scholarships--tuition.html	EAP|EE|MENA|SCA|SSA
Angus-Sawise Scholarships in Science and Engineering for African Women www.sawise.uct.ac.za/sawise/scholarships	SSA
Anne van den Ban Scholarships for Developing Countries at Wageningen University www.wur.nl/en/Benefactors/More-information-1/For-Applicants/Anne-van-den-Ban-Fund.htm	EAP|MENA|SCA|SSA
ANU International University Scholarship: www.anu.edu.au/students/scholarships	EAP|EE|MENA|SCA|SSA|WH
Agence Universitaire de la Francophonie (AUF) scholarship programs: https://www.auf.org/ressources-et-services/bourses/	

Scholarship programs or providing/host organizations (continued)	World regions
APLP Fellowships for International Students (Asia Pacific): www.eastwestcenter.org/education/aplp	EAP
ARES Scholarships in Belgium for Developing Countries: https://www.ares-ac.be/en/cooperation-au-developpement/scholarships	EAP|MENA|SCA|SSA
ARSA Travel Scholarships for Commonwealth Citizens http://arsa.org.au/index.php?Public_TravelScholarship	EAP|EE|MENA|SCA|SSA|WH
ASEAN Foundation Scholarships in Development, Environment, and IT for ASEAN Nationals www.aseanfoundation.org/newsroom/asean-foundation-research-scholarship	EAP|SCA
ASEAN Scholarships for Indonesian Youth - Singapore Ministry of Education www.moe.gov.sg/admissions/scholarships/asean/indonesia	EAP|SCA
Asian Cultural Council http: www.asianculturalcouncil.org/programs.html#acc	EAP|SCA
Asian Development Bank (ADB) - Japan Scholarship Program http: www.adb.org/JSP/default.asp	EAP|SCA
Association for International Agriculture and Rural Development (AIARD) http://aiard.org/index.htm	EAP|MENA|SCA|SSA
Association of African Universities: https://blog.aau.org/?s=scholarship	MENA|SSA
Australia Awards Fellowships: http://dfat.gov.au/people-to-people/australia-awards/pages/australia-awards-fellowships.aspx	EAP|EE|MENA|SCA|SSA|WH
Australia Awards Masters Scholarships for Africa: www.australiaawardsafrica.org	SSA
Australian Government Research Training Program (AGRTP) www.anu.edu.au/students/scholarships/international-postgraduate-research-scholarship-iprs	EAP|MENA|SCA|SSA
Austrian Partnership Programme in Higher Education and Research for Development (APPEAR): https://appear.at/en/	EAP|EE|MENA|SCA|SSA|WH
Barcelona GSE Tuition Fee Waivers for Master's Program in Economics, Finance, and Data Science: www.barcelonagse.eu/study/financial-aid	EAP|EE|MENA|SCA|SSA|WH
Bath Spa University Vice Chancellor's International Scholarship www.bathspa.ac.uk/students/student-finance/scholarships-and-funding	EAP|EE|MENA|SCA|SSA|WH
Berea College Scholarships: www.berea.edu/admissions/applying-for-admission/international-students	EAP|EE|MENA|SCA|SSA|WH
Bertha Scholarships for Social Innovators in Africa: www.gsb.uct.ac.za/bc-scholarships	SSA
Bibliographical Society of America Fellowship Program http: www.bibsocamer.org/fellows.htm Short-term	WH
Bliss Prize Fellowship http: www.doaks.org/Blissprize. html	EAP|EE|MENA|SCA|SSA|WH
Boren international scholarships for US students: https://www.borenawards.org/	WH

Scholarship programs or providing/host organizations (continued)	World regions
Danish Government Scholarships at University College of Northern Denmark www.ucn.dk/english/programmes-and-courses/admission/tuition-for-non-eu/non-eea-citizens/danish-government-scholarships	EAP|EE|MENA|SCA|SSA|WH
Danish State Tuition Fee Waivers and Scholarships at Roskilde University https://ruc.dk/en/step-5-tuition-fees-tuition-fee-waivers-and-scholarships	EAP|EE|MENA|SCA|SSA|WH
Dartmouth College Scholarships: www.dartmouth.edu/~scholarship/internationalstudents.html	EAP|EE|MENA|SCA|SSA|WH
Davis-Putter Scholarships: www.davisputter.org/	EAP|EE|MENA|SCA|SSA|WH
Denmark-India Innovation Challenge https://studentcompetitions.com/competitions/denmark-india-innovation-challenge	EAP|EE
Desmond Tutu's Masters Scholarships for Africans at the University of Edinburgh www.ed.ac.uk/student-funding/postgraduate/international/humanities/divinity/tutu	SSA
Deutschland Stipendium National Scholarship Program: www.deutschlandstipendium.de/de/2319.php	EAP|EE|MENA|SCA|SSA|WH
Domus Academy Scholarship Competition: www.domusacademy.com/en/category/scholarship	EAP|EE|MENA|SCA|SSA|WH
DRD PhD Scholarships in International Development Studies for Sub-Saharan Africans www.drd-sa.org/index.php/scholarships-in-development-studies.html	SSA
East Tennessee State University: www.etsu.edu/honors/international/internationalstudentscholarships/	EAP|EE|MENA|SCA|SSA|WH
Echoing Green Foundation Fellowships: www.echoinggreen.org/index.cfm?fuseaction=Page.viewPage&pageId=411	EAP|EE|MENA|SCA|SSA|WH
Ecowas Mobility Scholarship http://www.ecowas.int/academic_mobilty_programme/?lang=fr	SSA
Edinburgh Global Development Academy Scholarships www.ed.ac.uk/global-development/postgraduate/scholarships	EAP|EE|MENA|SCA|SSA|WH
EDISU Piemonte Scholarships www.edisu.piemonte.it/en/services/scholarships-and-other-grants/scholarship	EAP|MENA|SCA|SSA
Edmund S. Muskie Ph.D. Fellowship http://www.americancouncils.org/program.asp?PageID=121&ProgramID=23	EAP|EE|MENA|SCA|SSA|WH
Eiffel Excellence Scholarship Program: www.campusfrance.org/en/EIFFEL	EAP|MENA|SCA|SSA|WH
Eira Francis Davies Scholarship at Swansea University www.swansea.ac.uk/international/students/fees-and-funding/eira-davies-scholarship/	EAP|EE|MENA|SCA|SSA|WH
Eugen Ionescu scholarship program https://ri.uvt.ro/eugen-ionescu-doctoral-and-postdoctoral-scholarships/?lang=en	EAP|EE

Scholarship programs or providing/host organizations (continued)	World regions
China Scholarship Council: http://en.csc.edu.cn/	EAP|EE|MENA|SCA|SSA|WH
China Times Cultural Foundation Scholarships: www.chinesestudies.hawaii.edu/funding/scholarships/china_times.htm	EAP|EE|MENA|SCA|SSA|WH
Christine Mirzayan Science & Technology Policy Graduate Fellowship Program www7.nationalacademies.org/policyfellows/	EAP|EE|MENA|SCA|SSA|WH
CIMO Doctoral Fellowships in Finland: http://www.cimo.fi/programmes/cimo_ scholarships	EAP|EE|MENA|SCA|SSA|WH
Columbia College Scholarships: www.ccis.edu/offices/international/admissions/scholarships.aspx	EAP|EE|MENA|SCA|SSA|WH
Commonwealth Online Global Health Scholarships at University of Edinburgh www.ed.ac.uk/student-funding/postgraduate/e-learning/commglobalhealth	EAP|EE|MENA|SCA|SSA|WH
Commonwealth Scholarship for Integrative Sciences and Engineering at NUS Graduate School www.nus.edu.sg/ngs/scholarships.html	EAP|EE|MENA|SCA|SSA|WH
Commonwealth Scholarships: http://cscuk.dfid.gov.uk/apply/scholarships-developing-cw	EAP|EE|MENA|SCA|SSA|WH
Commonwealth Shared Scholarship Scheme at UK Universities http://cscuk.dfid.gov.uk/apply/shared-scholarships/	EAP|EE|MENA|SCA|SSA|WH
Conicyt National Scholarship in Chile: www.conicyt.cl/becasconicyt/formation-of-advanced-human-capital-program/	
Cosmos Club Foundation Grants in Aid to Young Scholars: www.cosmosclubfoundation.org/scholars	EAP|EE|MENA|SCA|SSA|WH
Council for the Development of Social Science Research in Africa (CODESRIA) www.codesria.org/spip.php?rubrique68	MENA|SSA
CSC–UWA Joint PhD Scholarships for Chinese Students: www.scholarships.uwa.edu.au/search?id=455	EAP
SOAS University of London Scholarship: www.soas.ac.uk/registry/scholarships	EAP|EE|MENA|SCA|SSA|WH
Curtin University International Research Scholarships https://scholarships.curtin.edu.au/search#/?Nationality=NA,International&CourseType=Undergraduate&keyword=	EAP|MENA|SCA|SSA|
Czech Government Scholarships for Developing Country Students www.msmt.cz/eu-and-international-affairs/government-scholarships-developing-countries?lang=2	EAP|MENA|SCA|SSA
DAAD German Academic Exchange Service and Scholarships: https://www.daad.de/deutschland/stipendium/datenbank/en/21148-scholarship-database/	EAP|EE|MENA|SCA|SSA|WH
DAAD-OSI Scholarships for the Balkans and Central Asia	EAP|EE|SCA

Scholarship programs or providing/host organizations (continued)	World regions
Eldred-Waverley Scholarship at Linacre College, Oxford: www.linacre.ox.ac.uk/prospective-students/scholarships/eldred-scholarship	EAP|MENA|SCA|SSA|WH
Elie Wiesel Prize in Ethics http://www.eliewieselfoundation.org/EthicsPrize/information.html	EAP|EE|MENA|SCA|SSA|WH
Elizabeth Greenshields Foundation Grant for Artists www.calarts.edu/~stdafrs/web/greenshields.html	EAP|EE|MENA|SCA|SSA|WH
Emerging Economy Fellowships at Wharton Business School https://mba.wharton.upenn.edu/tuition-financial-aid/	EAP|MENA|SCA|SSA
Emily Boutmy Scholarships for International Students at Sciences Po (France) http://formation.sciences-po.fr/en/contenu/the-emile-boutmy-scholarship	EAP|MENA|SCA|SSA
Emory College Scholarships: http://apply.emory.edu/apply/scholar.php	EAP|EE|MENA|SCA|SSA|WH
Endeavour Postgraduate Awards: https://internationaleducation.gov.au/endeavour	EAP|EE|MENA|SCA|SSA|WH
ENS International Selection Scholarships (France) www.ens.fr/en/academics/admissions/international-selection	EAP|EE|MENA|SCA|SSA|WH
Environmental Research and Education Foundation http://www.erefdn.org/scholar.html	EAP|EE|MENA|SCA|SSA|WH
EPFL Excellence Fellowships: https://master.epfl.ch/excellence-fellowships	EAP|EE|MENA|SCA|SSA|WH
Erasmus Mundus Joint Master Degree Scholarships in Media Arts Cultures: www.mediaartscultures.eu/mediaac/	EE
Erasmus Mundus Scholarships for International Students: http://eacea.ec.europa.eu/erasmus_mundus/funding/scholarships_students_academics_en.php	EE
Erasmus Mundus Scholarships in Coastal and Marine Engineering and Management: www.ntnu.edu/studies/mscomem	EE
Erik Bleumink Scholarships at University of Groningen (Netherlands) www.rug.nl/education/international-students/financial-matters/ericbleumink	EAP|EE|MENA|SCA|SSA|WH
ESMT Women's Academic Scholarships www.esmt.org/executive-education/advanced-management-programs/esmt-womens-scholarship	EAP|MENA|SCA|SSA|WH
ETH Excellence Scholarships (Switzerland): www.ethz.ch/students/en/studies/financial/scholarships/excellencescholarship.html	EAP|MENA|SCA|SSA|WH
Eurasian Undergraduate Exchange Program (UGRAD): www.irex.org/programs/ugrad/index.asp	EE
EUREKA SD Partnership scholarships for European to study in Latin America http://www.eureka-sd-project.eu/general_information	EE

Scholarship programs or providing/host organizations (continued)	World regions
EWC Graduate Degree Scholarships for Asia and the Pacific: www.eastwestcenter.org/scholarships-fellowships	EAP|SCA
Exploration Fund of the Explorers Club: https://explorers.org/expeditions/funding/expedition_grants	EAP|EE|MENA|SCA|SSA|WH
Ferguson Scholarships for Africans at SOAS London www.soas.ac.uk/registry/scholarships/ferguson-scholarships.html	MENA|SSA
Florence Congleton Scholarships for African Women at University of Birmingham www.birmingham.ac.uk/schools/education/scholarships/florence-congleton-scholarship-award.aspx	SSA
Ford Foundation www.fordfoundation.org/the-latest/ford-live-events/international-fellowships-program-the-power-of-many/	EAP|EE|MENA|SCA|SSA|WH
U.S. and foreign Fulbright Programs https://eca.state.gov/fulbright/fulbright-programs/program-summaries	EAP|EE|MENA|SCA|SSA|WH
Foundation Rainbow Bridge MBA Scholarships for African and Asian Women www.mba.hec.edu/Fees-Funding/Scholarships/Fondation-Rainbow-Bridge	EAP|MENA|SCA|SSA
French Ministry of Foreign and European Affairs www.diplomatie.gouv.fr/en/coming-to-france/studying-in-france/finance-your-studies-scholarships/	EAP|EE|MENA|SCA|SSA|WH
Full Distance Learning Scholarships for East and South African Students at London South Bank University (Commonwealth scholarships) http://cscuk.dfid.gov.uk/apply/distance-learning/courses/	MENA|SSA
Full-Fee Scholarships for Africans at Loughborough University www.lboro.ac.uk/students/finance/international/scholarships	SSA
Future Global Leaders Scholarship at Coventry University www.coventry.ac.uk/international-students-hub/new-students/international-scholarships-and-discounts	EAP|EE|MENA|SCA|SSA|WH
Future Leaders of Sustainability Masters Distinction Scholarship at University of Exeter www.exeter.ac.uk/postgraduate/money/fundingsearch/awarddetails/?id=2466	EAP|EE|MENA|SCA|SSA|WH
Gates Cambridge Scholarships http://www.gates.scholarships.cam.ac.uk/ www.gatescambridge.org	EAP|EE|MENA|SCA|SSA|WH
GeTMA Scholarships for International Students in Turkey/Germany www.daad.de/deutschland/studienangebote/international-programmes/en/	EAP|EE|MENA|SCA|SSA|WH
Glamour Magazine's Top Ten College Women Competition: www.glamour.com/story/top-college-women-app	EAP|EE|MENA|SCA|SSA|WH
Global Business Scholarship at S P Jain School of Global Management www.spjain.org/programs/undergraduate/scholarship	EAP|EE|MENA|SCA|SSA|WH

Scholarship programs or providing/host organizations (continued)	World regions
Global Undergraduate Exchange Program (Global UGRAD) https://exchanges.state.gov/non-us/program/global-undergraduate-exchange-program-global-ugrad	EAP|EE|MENA|SCA|SSA|WH
Goldman Sachs Global Leaders Program http://www.gs.com/our_firm/our_culture/social_responsibility/gs_foundation/index.html	EAP|EE|MENA|SCA|SSA|WH
Governance for Development in Africa Scholarships at SOAS University of London: www.soas.ac.uk/gdai/	SSA
Government of Flanders Master Mind Scholarships for International Students www.flandershouse.org/master-mind-scholarships	EAP|MENA|SCA|SSA|WH
Graça Machel Scholarships for South African Women www.canoncollins.org.uk/apply/scholarship/grac%CC%A7a-machel-scholarships	SSA
Guest Sweden Masters Scholarships for Developing Countries https://studyinsweden.se/scholarships/swedish-institute-scholarships/	EAP|MENA|SCA|SSA
Hedley Bull Scholarships in International Affairs at Australian National University www.anu.edu.au/students/scholarships/hedley-bull-scholarship	EAP|EE|MENA|SCA|SSA|WH
Heinrich Boll Scholarships in Germany for International Students www.boell.de/en/scholarships-application	EAP|EE|MENA|SCA|SSA|WH
Hellenic Scholarship Program for Foreign Students from Developing Countries www.ihu.edu.gr/index.php/financial-assistance.html	EAP|MENA|SCA|SSA
Hellenic Times Scholarship Fund: http://www.htsfund.org/guidelines.html	EAP|EE|MENA|SCA|SSA|WH
Herbert Scoville Jr. Peace Fellowships http://www.clw.org/pub/clw/scoville/index.html	EAP|EE|MENA|SCA|SSA|WH
Hessnatur Scholarships: http://esmod.de/en/hessnatur-foundation-scholarship-2017/	EAP|EE|MENA|SCA|SSA|WH
Holland Scholarship for Non-EEA International Students www.studyinholland.nl/scholarships/holland-scholarship	EAP|MENA|SCA|SSA|WH
Hong Kong PhD Fellowship Scheme for International Students: ttps://cerg1.ugc.edu.hk/hkpfs/index.html	EAP|EE|MENA|SCA|SSA|WH
IBrasil Study in Brazil Scholarship: http://www.ibrasilmundus.eu/	EAP|EE|MENA|SCA|SSA|WH
IFCO Full Scholarship Program-Study medicine in Cuba https://ifconews.org/medical-school/frequently-asked-questions/	SSA|WH
International Dissertation Field Research Fellowships http://www.ssrc.org/programs/idrf/	EAP|EE|MENA|SCA|SSA|WH
International Foundation for Science: http://www.ifs.se/	EAP|EE|MENA|SCA|SSA|WH

Scholarship programs or providing/host organizations (continued)	World regions
International Fulbright Science and Technology Scholarships: http://fulbrightscienceandtech.org/about/the-fulbright-st-program/	EAP|EE|MENA|SCA|SSA|WH
International Leader of Tomorrow Award at University of British Columbia (Canada) http://you.ubc.ca/financial-planning/scholarships-awards-international-students/	EAP|EE|MENA|SCA|SSA|WH
International Masters Scholarships for Non-EU students at University of Arts London: http://www.arts.ac.uk/study-at-ual/student-fees--funding/scholarships-search/	EAP|MENA|SCA|SSA|WH
International Peace Studies Scholarships for Asians Nippon Foundation/Univ. of Peace https://www.upeace.org/academic/partnership-programmes/asia-peacebuilders-scholarship	EAP|SCA
International PhD Fellowships at Max Planck Research School for Ultrafast Imaging & Structural https://www.mpsd.mpg.de/IMPRS	EAP|EE|MENA|SCA|SSA|WH
International Summer School Scholarships at University of Oslo: https://www.uio.no/english/studies/summerschool/admission/scholarships/	EAP|EE|MENA|SCA|SSA|WH
International Undergraduate Scholarships at University of Queensland: https://scholarships.uq.edu.au/	EAP|EE|MENA|SCA|SSA|WH
INTO International Foundation Scholarships at University of East Anglia www.intostudy.com/en-gb/universities/university-of-east-anglia/studying/scholarships	EAP|EE|MENA|SCA|SSA|WH
ISH/UAL Graduate Scholarships for International Students https://ish.org.uk/student-zone/scholarship/available-scholarships/	EAP|EE|MENA|SCA|SSA|WH
ISH-London Met Scholarship Scheme: www.londonmet.ac.uk/applying/funding-your-studies/scholarships/	EAP|EE|MENA|SCA|SSA|WH
Israeli Government Scholarships for International Students http://mfa.gov.il/MFA/AboutTheMinistry/Documents/scholarshipinstructions.pdf	EAP|EE|MENA|SCA|SSA|WH
ISS PhD fellowships in Development Studies: https://www.iss.nl/prospective_students/fellowships/	EAP|EE|MENA|SCA|SSA|WH
Italian Government Bursaries for Foreign Students (Italy) www.esteri.it/mae/en/ministero/servizi/stranieri/opportunita/borsestudio_stranieri.html	EAP|EE|MENA|SCA|SSA|WH
IWC Masters Scholarships for International Students www.watercentre.org/education/programs/scholarships/iwc-scholarships	EAP|EE|MENA|SCA|SSA|WH
J. W. Saxe Memorial Fund http://www.jwsaxefund.org/memorialfund.html	EAP|EE|MENA|SCA|SSA|WH
Jack Kent Cooke Graduate Scholarships http://www.jackkentcookefoundation.org/jkcf_web/content.aspx?page=SchProg	EAP|EE|MENA|SCA|SSA|WH

Scholarship programs or providing/host organizations (continued)	World regions
Japan HR Development Scholarships (JDS) for Developing Countries in Asia: http://jds-scholarship.org/	EAP|SCA
Japan-IMF Scholarship Program for Advanced Studies: www.imf.org/external/np/ta/jaa/jfsc.htm	EAP|SCA
Japan-IMF Scholarships for Asia: www.imf.org/external/oap/schol.htm	EAP|SCA
JFUNU Scholarships for MSc in Sustainability Program for Developing Country Students https://ias.unu.edu/en/admissions/degrees/msc-in-sustainability-2017.html#scholarships	EAP|MENA|SCA|SSA
JNCASR–COSTED Fellowships for Developing Countries: http://www.jncasr.ac.in/fe/	EAP|MENA|SCA|SSA|WH
John Bayliss Radio Scholarship http://www.baylissfoundation.org/radio.html	EAP|EE|MENA|SCA|SSA|WH
Josephine de Karman Scholarships http://www.dekarman.org	EAP|EE|MENA|SCA|SSA|WH
Kadir Has University Undergraduate Scholarships in Turkey for International Students http://international.khas.edu.tr/22/tuition-fees	EAP|EE|MENA|SCA|SSA|WH
Kate Neal Kinley Memorial Fellowship http://www.faa.uiuc.edu/about_faa/funding_opportunities.html	EAP|EE|MENA|SCA|SSA|WH
Kennis ontwikkelings programma ('KOP) www.logavak.nl/aanbod/19/223/990/kop-opleiding-debabyspecialistisch-coach	EAP|EE|MENA|SCA|SSA|WH
King Faisal Foundation Scholarship http://www.kff.com/english/kff/ea/ss/bfullkffeass.htm	EAP|EE|MENA|SCA|SSA|WH
Kofi Annan MBA Scholarships for Developing Country Students: goo.gl/G7zk2e	EAP|EE|MENA|SCA|SSA|WH
Korean Government Scholarships: www.niied.go.kr/eng/contents.do?contentsNo=78&menuNo=349	EAP|EE|MENA|SCA|SSA|WH
KTH Tuition Fee Waiver for Non-EU Students www.kth.se/en/studies/master/fees-funding/kth-scholarship-1.72827	EAP|MENA|SCA|SSA|WH
KUT PhD Scholarships in Engineering for International Students https://www.kochi-tech.ac.jp/english/admission/ssp/guideline.html	EAP|EE|MENA|SCA|SSA|WH
La Trobe Academic Excellence Scholarships for International Students www.latrobe.edu.au/international/fees-and-scholarships	EAP|EE|MENA|SCA|SSA|WH
Lalji PfAL Scholarship for Sub-Saharan Africans at London School of Economics	SSA
LANL-CBNU Engineering Institute Graduate and Post Doc Scholarships in Korea	EAP|EE|MENA|SCA|SSA|WH
Leader of the Pack Scholarships http://www.ncsu.edu/csleps/leadership/lop.htm	EAP|EE|MENA|SCA|SSA|WH
Leadership and Advocacy Fellowship Program for Women in Africa	SSA
Lee Kong Chian Graduate Scholarships at National University of Singapore	EAP|EE|MENA|SCA|SSA|WH
Leeds International Research Scholarships	EAP|MENA|SCA|SSA|WH

Scholarship programs or providing/host organizations (continued)	World regions
Leiden University Excellence Scholarships (Netherlands)www.universiteitleiden.nl/onderwijs/masters	EAP|EE|MENA|SCA|SSA|WH
Lindbergh Grants http://www.lindberghfoundation.org/grants/	EAP|EE|MENA|SCA|SSA|WH
LJMU Roscoe International Scholarship www.ljmu.ac.uk/applicant-login/scholarships-for-international-applicants	EAP|EE|MENA|SCA|SSA|WH
Lord Walston Scholarships for Africans at University of East Anglia www.uea.ac.uk/study/postgraduate/scholarships	EAP|EE|MENA|SCA|SSA|WH
Loughborough University Graduate School Development Trust Africa Scholarships www.lboro.ac.uk/students/finance/international/additionalinfo-africa/	SSA
Louis Dreyfus-Weidenfeld and Hoffmann Scholarship and Leadership Programme at Oxford: http://whtrust.org/scholarships/how-to-apply/	EAP|MENA|SCA|SSA|WH
Lund University Global Scholarships for Non-EU/EEA Students (Sweden) www.lunduniversity.lu.se/international-admission/bachelors-masters-studies/scholarships-awards/lund-university-global	EE
Lund University's 350th Jubilee Scholarship http://www.lund350scholarship.com/	EAP|EE|MENA|SCA|SSA|WH
M.A. Cartland Shackford Medical Fellowship http://www.wellesley.edu/CWS/students/wellfs.html	EAP|EE|MENA|SCA|SSA|WH
Maastricht University Holland High Potential Scholarships for International Students www.maastrichtuniversity.nl/support/your-studies-begin/coming-maastricht-university-abroad/scholarships/maastricht-university	EAP|MENA|SCA|SSA|WH
MacDowell Colony Residencies http://www.macdowellcolony.org/index.html.	EAP|MENA|SCA|SSA|WH
Macquarie Vice-Chancellor's International Scholarships: www.mq.edu.au/study/international-students/staging/details/vcis	EAP|MENA|SCA|SSA|WH
Malaysia International Scholarships (MIS): https://biasiswa.mohe.gov.my/INTER/index.php	EAP|EE|MENA|SCA|SSA|WH
Margaret McNamara Memorial Fund Grants http://www.gwu.edu/~fellows/mmmf.html	EAP|EE|MENA|SCA|SSA|WH
Marie Curie International Incoming Fellowships (IIF) for Developing Countries https://ec.europa.eu/research/mariecurieactions/about_en	EAP|MENA|SCA|SSA
MasterCard Foundation Scholarship Program for Africans: www.mastercardfdn.org/scholars-program/	SSA
Masters in Engineering Geology Scholarships at the University of Leeds (UK) http://www.see.leeds.ac.uk/admissions-and-study/masters-degrees/admissions-and-study/fees-scholarships/	EAP|MENA|SCA|SSA|WH
Masters Scholarships at CEU School of Public Policy: https://spp.ceu.edu/financial-aid	EAP|EE|MENA|SCA|SSA|WH

Scholarship programs or providing/host organizations (continued)	World regions
Mayo Summer Undergraduate Research Fellowship (SURF) Program http://www.mayo.edu/mgs/surf.html	EAP|EE|MENA|SCA|SSA|WH
MBA Tuition Fee Waiver Competition at MIP Politecnico di Milano Graduate School of Business http://www.mip.polimi.it/en/academics/people-and-careers/mba-and-executive-mba/international-full-time-mba/financial-aid/	EAP|MENA|SCA|SSA|WH
Melbourne Human Rights Scholarships: https://studenteforms.app.unimelb.edu.au/apex/f?p=153:2:0:::2:P2_ID:221	EAP|EE|MENA|SCA|SSA|WH
Melbourne Research Scholarships (Australia): http://services.unimelb.edu.au/scholarships/research	EAP|EE|MENA|SCA|SSA|WH
MENA Scholarship Programme (MSP) for Professionals from Middle East and North Africa www.un-ihe.org/middle-east-and-north-africa-scholarship-programme-msp	MENA
Mexican Government Scholarships: https://www.gob.mx/amexcid/acciones-y-programas/becas-para-extranjeros-29785	EAP|EE|MENA|SCA|SSA|WH
Mexico Multicultural Nation University Scholarship at Universidad Nacional Autónoma de México (UNAM)for indigenous students worldwide: http://www.posgrado.unam.mx/en/foreigners-unam to gain funding to study in Mexico at the	EAP|MENA|SCA|SSA|WH
Michigan State University International Scholarships: https://admissions.msu.edu/cost-aid/merit-based-aid/freshman/international.aspx	EAP|EE|MENA|SCA|SSA
Microsoft Research Women's Fellowship Program: www.microsoft.com/en-us/research/academic-program/womens-fellowship-program/	EAP|EE|MENA|SCA|SSA|WH
Microsoft Scholarships http://www.microsoft.com/college/scholarships	EAP|EE|MENA|SCA|SSA|WH
Mid Sweden University Tuition Fee Scholarships: www.miun.se/en/education/programmes/Fees-and-scholarships/Scholarship/	EAP|EE|MENA|SCA|SSA|WH
MMMF Educational Grants in South Africa for Women from Developing Countries: http://www.mmeg.org/	SSA
Mo Ibrahim Foundation Scholarship for Sub-Saharan Africans http://mo.ibrahim.foundation/fellowships/scholarships/	SSA
Monash International Scholarships (Australia): https://www.monash.edu/students/scholarships/current/international	EAP|MENA|SCA|SSA|
Monbukagakusho Scholarship http://www.u-tokyo.ac.jp/en/prospective-students/mext_scholarship.html	
MRes in Climate and Atmospheric Science Scholarships at University of Leeds http://www.see.leeds.ac.uk/admissions-and-study/masters-degrees/admissions-and-study/fees-scholarships/scholarships/	EAP|MENA|SCA|SSA|WH
MTN Solution Space Scholarships for Africans: http://www.gsb.uct.ac.za/solution-space-scholarships	MENA|SSA

Scholarship programs or providing/host organizations (continued)	World regions
NABA Calls for International Talents: http://competition.naba.it/	EAP|MENA|SCA|SSA|WH
NASP/GSSPS PhD Scholarships in Social and Political Sciences in Italy: http://www.nasp.eu/training/scholarships-financial-aids.html	EAP|MENA|SCA|SSA|WH
National University of Singapore NUS Graduate Student Fellowships for Asians: https://ari.nus.edu.sg/Page/AGSF2017	
National Association of Black Journalists (NABJ) Scholarships http://www.nabj.org/programs/scholarships/	SSA|WH
National Institutes of Health (NIH) – University of Pennsylvania Advanced Immunology Scholars http://gpp.nih.gov/Applicants/ProspectiveStudents/Immunology/	EAP|EE|MENA|SCA|SSA|WH
Nelson Mandela Scholarships http://www.nelsonmandelascholarship.co.za	SSA
Nestle MBA Scholarships for Women from Developing Countries: https://owsd.net/switzerland-nestle-mba-scholarships	EAP|MENA|SCA|SSA|WH
Netherlands Fellowship Program NUFFIC: www.nuffic.nl/en/scholarships/copy_of_nfp-individual-scholarships	EAP|MENA|SCA|SSA|WH
New York University Wagner Scholarships: https://wagner.nyu.edu/admissions/financial-aid/scholarships	EAP|EE|MENA|SCA|SSA|WH
New Zealand Aid Programme Scholarships for International Students https://www.mfat.govt.nz/en/aid-and-development/scholarships/types-of-scholarships	EAP|EE|MENA|SCA|SSA|WH
New Zealand International Doctoral Research Scholarships https://enz.govt.nz/support/funding/scholarships/new-zealand-international-doctoral-research-scholarships	EAP|EE|MENA|SCA|SSA|WH
New Zealand–ASEAN Scholar Awards https://www.auckland.ac.nz/en/study/international-students/scholarships-loans-and-funding/development-scholarships/nz-asean-scolar-awards.html	EAP|SCA
Newton's List: http://newtonslist.crdfglobal.org/opportunity-search	EAP|EE|MENA|SCA|SSA|WH
Nippon Foundation Fellowships for Asian Public Intellectuals: http://www.api-fellowships.org/body/	EAP|SCA
Norwegian Agency for Development Cooperation (Norad): https://www.norad.no/en/front/funding/	EAP|MENA|SCA|SSA
Norwegian Centre for International Cooperation in Education (SIU) www.studyinnorway.no/study-in-norway/Scholarships	EAP|MENA|SCA|SSA|WH
Nottingham Developing Solutions Scholarships http://www.nottingham.ac.uk/studywithus/international-applicants/scholarships-fees-and-finance/scholarships/scholarshipdetails/scholarshipapplicationpage.aspx	EAP|MENA|SCA|SSA|WH
Nottingham Trent University Science Scholarships for Non-EU Students www.ntu.ac.uk/study-and-courses/international/fees-and-scholarships/scholarships	EAP|MENA|SCA|SSA|WH

Scholarship programs or providing/host organizations (continued)	World regions
Nottingham University Business School PhD Scholarships: https://www.nottingham.ac.uk/business/programmes/phd/fees-and-scholarships.aspx	EAP|MENA|SCA|SSA|WH
Nottingham Vice-Chancellor's International Scholarship for Research Excellence http://www.nottingham.ac.uk/pgstudy/funding/vice-chancellors-scholarships-for-research-excellence.aspx	EAP|MENA|SCA|SSA|WH
NYU Wagner Public Service Fellowships for African Women https://wagner.nyu.edu/admissions/financial-aid/fellowships/awpsf	SSA
OAS Organization of American States Scholarships http: www.oas.org/en/scholarships/	WH
OCIS Scholarships for Muslims from Developing Countries http://www.oxcis.ac.uk/ocisoxfordschol.html	EAP|EE|MENA|SCA|SSA|WH
Open Society Foundations Scholarship: www.opensocietyfoundations.org/about/programs/scholarship-programs	MENA|SSA
Oppenheimer Fund Scholarships at University of Oxford https://www.ox.ac.uk/about/international-oxford/resources-staff-and-students/oppenheimer-fund-scholarships?wssl=1	EAP|MENA|SCA|SSA|WH
Oregon University Scholarships: https://admissions.uoregon.edu/international/apply/scholarship	EAP|EE|MENA|SCA|SSA|WH
Oslo Peace Scholarship at Australian National University http://www.anu.edu.au/students/scholarships	EAP|MENA|SCA|SSA|WH
Overseas Research Students Award Scheme http://www.universitiesuk.ac.uk/ors	EAP|MENA|SCA|SSA|WH
Patrick Charnon Memorial Scholarship: http://www.wm.edu/sites/scholarships/scholarshipsfellowshipsawards/scholarshipPages/charnon/index.php	EAP|EE|MENA|SCA|SSA|WH
Peace Scholar Dissertation Fellowship http://www.usip.org/fellows/scholars.html	EAP|EE|MENA|SCA|SSA|WH
PEO International Peace Scholarships for Women https://www.peointernational.org/about-peo-international-peace-scholarship-ips	EAP|EE|MENA|SCA|SSA|WH
Peterhouse Research Studentships, University of Cambridge http://www.pet.cam.ac.uk/admissions/research-studentships.html	EAP|MENA|SCA|SSA|WH
PhD Fellowships for Developing Countries at University of Groningen: http://www.rug.nl/education/international-students/financial-matters/ericbleumink	EAP|MENA|SCA|SSA
PhD Scholarships for Developing Countries at the Intl Center for Dvpment and Decent Work (ICDD) https://www.uni-kassel.de/einrichtungen/international/international-center-for-development-and-decent-work-icdd/home.html	EAP|EE|MENA|SCA|SSA|WH
Phi Kappa Phi Fellowships http://www.phikappaphi.org/Web/Scholarships/graduatefellowship.html	EAP|EE|MENA|SCA|SSA|WH

Scholarship programs or providing/host organizations (continued)	World regions
Phillips Exeter Academy Fellowships & Internships http://www.exeter.edu/about_us/about_us_490.asp	
Politecnico de Milano Merit-Based Scholarships for International Students http://www.polinternational.polimi.it/how-to-apply/laurea-magistrale/scholarships/	
Postgraduate Fellowships for Women Scientists from Sub-Saharan Africa and Least Developed Count https://owsd.net/career-development/phd-fellowship	SSA
Professor Arthur Li Scholarship at the University of the West of England http://www1.uwe.ac.uk/students/feesandfunding/fundingandscholarships/internationalstudentfunding.aspx	EAP|MENA|SCA|SSA|WH
Radboud Scholarship Programme for International Students(Netherlands) http://www.ru.nl/english/education/masters-programmes/international-masters-students/financial-matters/scholarships-grants/	EAP|MENA|SCA|SSA|WH
Rainforest Alliance Kleinhans Fellowships: http://www.rainforest-alliance.org/careers/kleinhans-fellowship	EAP|EE|MENA|SCA|SSA WH
Ray Tongue Scholarships for Asian English Teachers (IATEFL Conference): https://conference.iatefl.org/scholarships.html	EAP|SCA
Reach Oxford Scholarships for Developing Country Students www.ox.ac.uk/admissions/undergraduate/fees-and-funding/oxford-support/reach-oxford-scholarship	EAP|MENA|SCA|SSA|WH
Rhodes Scholarships for Non-U.S. Citizens http://www.rhodesscholar.org	EAP|EE|MENA|SCA|SSA,|WH
Rhodes Scholarships in Oxford University for Southern Africans https://www.rhodeshouse.ox.ac.uk/scholarship/how-to-apply-for-a-rhodes-scholarship/?selectedRegion=7b65d124-0520-4aec-928b-957defca29ba	SSA
Roberto Rocca international scholarships to study in Latin America http://www.robertorocca.org/en/scholarships.aspx	EAP|EE|MENA|SCA|SSA|WH
Roehampton University Sacred Heart (RUSH) Scholarships for International Students https://www.roehampton.ac.uk/graduate-school/funding/	EAP|EE|MENA|SCA|SSA|WH
Rotary Peace Fellowships -Study in: USA, Japan, UK, Australia, Sweden, Thailand https://www.rotary.org/en/our-programs/peace-fellowships	EAP|EE|MENA|SCA|SSA|WH
Ruth First Scholarships for Southern Africans at Durham University https://www.dur.ac.uk/postgraduate/finance/scholarships/ruthfirst/	SSA
S P Jain School of Global Management https://www.spjain.org/programs/undergraduate/scholarships	EAP|EE|MENA|SCA|SSA|WH
SAIA - Slovak Academic Information Agency Scholarships: https://www.saia.sk/en	EAP|MENA|SCA|SSA|WH
Samuel Huntington Public Service Fellowship Award https://www9.nationalgridus.com/masselectric/about_us/award.asp	EAP|EE|MENA|SCA|SSA|WH
SCG Foundation Scholarships in International Development at Chulalongkorn University: www.ids.polsci.chula.ac.th	EAP|MENA|SCA|SSA|WH

Scholarship programs or providing/host organizations (continued)	World regions
Schlumberger Cambridge Scholarships for student from developing countries: www.cambridgetrust.org/scholarships/scholarship/?award=18	EAP|EE|MENA|SCA|SSA|WH
Scholarship for the Global Management of Social Issues at Tilburg University https://www.tilburguniversity.edu/education/bachelors-programs/financial-matters/scholarships-and-grants/	EAP|EE|MENA|SCA|SSA|WH
Scholarships for International Students at University of Exeter http://www.exeter.ac.uk/studying/funding/international/	EAP|EE|MENA|SCA|SSA|WH
Schwarzman Scholars Program at Tsinghua University (China): http://www.schwarzmanscholars.org/	EAP|EE|MENA|SCA|SSA|WH
Science Leuven Scholarships for International Students https://wet.kuleuven.be/english/scienceatleuvenscholarship	EAP|EE|MENA|SCA|SSA|WH
SDA Bocconi MBA Scholarships www.sdabocconi.it/en/mba-executive-mba/full-time-mba/admissions/scholarships-funding#content	EAP|EE|MENA|SCA|SSA|WH
SEARCA Graduate Scholarships in Agriculture for Southeast Asians www.searca.org/index.php/component/content/article/26-scholarship-announcements/990-searca-graduate-scholarship-for-southeast-asians	EAP|EE|MENA|SCA|SSA|WH
Seaspace Scholarships http://www.wm.edu/sites/scholarships/scholarshipsfellowshipsawards/byPurpose/openToInternationalStudents/seaspace/index.php	EAP|EE|MENA|SCA|SSA|WH
Sheffield Hallam University Scholarship for international and European Union students: https://www.shu.ac.uk/international/fees-scholarships-and-discounts/scholarships-discounts-and-bursaries/transform-together-scholarships	EAP|EE|MENA|SCA|SSA|WH
Shuttleworth Fundation: https://www.shuttleworthfoundation.org/fellows/	EAP|EE|MENA|SCA|SSA|WH
Siam Cement Group Foundation https://beasiswaindo.com/scholarships/siam-cement-group-scg-foundation-scholarships-thailand/	EAP|SCA
Singapore Government Scholarships for Southeast Asians www.scp.gov.sg/content/scp/apply_now/eligibility.html	EAP|EE|MENA|SCA|SSA|WH
Singapore International Graduate Award: https://www.a-star.edu.sg/singa-award/	EAP|EE|MENA|SCA|SSA|WH
Skoll MBA Scholarships at Saïd Business School: https://www.sbs.ox.ac.uk/mba/funding/sbs	MENA|SCA|SSA|
Slovak Government Scholarships for Selected Developing Countries https://www.minedu.sk/scholarships-of-the-government-of-the-slovak-republic/	EAP||MENA|SCA|SSA|WH
Social Science Research Council: https://www.ssrc.org/fellowships/	EAP||MENA|SCA|SSA|WH
Society of Women Engineers http://www.societyofwomenengineers.org/scholarships/brochure.aspx	EAP|MENA|SCA|SSA|WH

Scholarship programs or providing/host organizations (continued)	World regions
South East Asian Studies Summer Institute (SEASSI) Tuition Fellowships http://seassi.wisc.edu/Admission/tf.htm	EAP|SCA
South Pacific and East Timor Scholarship Programs: http://pidp.eastwestcenter.org/pidp/Awards/spsaward1.htm http://	EAP|SCA
Southern African Scholarships at University of Edinburgh http://www.ed.ac.uk/student-funding/postgraduate/international	SSA
Spanish Government Scholarships for International Students http://www.aecid.es/EN/grants-and-assistantships	EAP|MENA|SCA|SSA
Spencer Foundation Dissertation Fellowship http://www.spencer.org/programs/index.htm	EAP|EE|MENA|SCA|SSA|WH
Sussex Chancellor's International Research Scholarships http://www.sussex.ac.uk/study/phd/fees-and-scholarships/scholarships/view/661	EAP|MENA|SCA|SSA|WH
Sustainability Masters Scholarships at University of Leeds http://www.see.leeds.ac.uk/admissions-and-study/masters-degrees/admissions-and-study/fees-scholarships/scholarships/	EAP|EE|MENA|SCA|SSA|WH
Swansea University International Excellence and Merit Scholarships http://www.swansea.ac.uk/international/students/fees-and-funding/scholarships/	EAP|EE|MENA|SCA|SSA|WH
Swedish International Development Agency (Sida) http://www.sida.se/English/get-involved/Sida-sponsored-scholarships/	EAP|EE|MENA|SCA|SSA|WH
Swedish Institute Study Scholarships (Sweden) https://eng.si.se/scholarship/the-swedish-institute-study-scholarships/	EAP|EE|MENA|SCA|SSA|WH
Swiss Benevolent Society of New York Scholarships http://www.swissbenevolentny.com/scholarshipprograms.htm	WH
Swiss Gov. Excellence Scholarships www.sbfi.admin.ch/sbfi/en/home/bildung/scholarships-and-grants.html	EAP|EE|MENA|SCA|SSA|WH
Taiwan Government Scholarships MOFA for International Students http://tafs.mofa.gov.tw/SchDetailed.aspx?loc=en&ItemId=15	EAP|EE|MENA|SCA|SSA|WH
Taiwan International Higher Education Scholarship Program http://www.icdf.org.tw/ct.asp?xItem=12505&CtNode=30316&mp=2	EAP|EE|MENA|SCA|SSA|WH
Talent for Governance Training Scholarships for Developing Countries http://thehagueacademy.com/tfg/talent-programme/why-who-what-and-how/	EAP|MENA|SCA|SSA|WH

Scholarship programs or providing/host organizations (continued)	World regions
Teaching Excellence and Achievement (TEA) Program https://www.irex.org/program/opportunity-international-teachers-teaching-excellence-and-achievement-tea-program	EAP|EE|MENA|SCA|SSA|WH
The "Invest your Talent in Italy" http://international.polito.it/financial_aid/politecnico_international_scholarships/invest_your_talent_in_italy	EAP|EE|MENA|SCA|SSA|WH (Azerbaijan, Colombia, Egypt, Ethiopia, Ghana, India, Indonesia, Iran, Kazakhstan, Mexico, Turkey, Tunisia, and Vietnam)
The African Capacity Building Foundation: https://www.acbf-pact.org/what-we-do/how-we-do-it/grants	SSA
The Andrew W. Mellon Foundation: https://mellon.org/programs/	EAP|EE|MENA|SCA|SSA|WH
The Bremen International Graduate School of Social Sciences (BIGSSS) Scholarships https://www.bigsss-bremen.de/	EAP|EE|MENA|SCA|SSA|WH
The Denys Holland Scholarship at University College London Scheme http://www.universitiesuk.ac.uk/ors	EAP|EE|MENA|SCA|SSA|WH
The East-West Center Graduate Degree Fellowship (students from Asia, the Pacific, and the U.S.) https://www.eastwestcenter.org/node/35148	EAP|SCA
The Glenmore Medical Postgraduate Scholarship at the University of Edinburgh http://www.ed.ac.uk/biomedical-sciences/postgraduate-studying/msc-science-communication/fees-and-funding	EAP|EE|MENA|SCA|SSA|WH
The Indian Council for Cultural Relations (ICCR): www.iccr.gov.in	EAP|EE|MENA|SCA|SSA|WH
The Rockefeller Foundation: https://www.rockefellerfoundation.org/our-work/grants/what-we-fund/	EAP|EE|MENA|SCA|SSA|WH
The Roothbert Fund Scholarship Program http://www.roothbertfund.org/scholarships.php	WH
The Swedish Scholarship Challenge 2014 for Chinese Students http://www.webforum.com/form/kthinternational/form.asp?sid=538443516	EAP
The University of Edinburgh Southern African Scholarships: http://www.ed.ac.uk/student-funding/postgraduate/international/region/africa	SSA
The University of Gothenburg International Scholarships (Sweeden): http://utbildning.gu.se/education/admissions/scholarships	EAP|EE|MENA|SCA|SSA|WH
The World Academy of Sciences (TWAS) for the advancement of science in developing countries https://twas.org/opportunities	EAP|MENA|SCA|SSA
The World Bank Scholarship Programs: http://www.worldbank.org/en/programs/scholarships	EAP|EE|MENA|SCA|SSA|WH

Scholarship programs or providing/host organizations (continued)	World regions
Tilburg University Academic Excellence Scholarships for International Students https://www.tilburguniversity.edu/education/masters-programmes/tuition-fees-scholarships/tiuscholarships	EAP|MENA|SCA|SSA|WH
Ting Hsin Scholarship at Waseda University https://www.waseda.jp/inst/scholarship/en/for-international-students	EAP|EE|MENA|SCA|SSA|WH
Trust Africa Grants: http://www.trustafrica.org/en/grants/grants-database	EAP|EE|MENA|SCA|SSA|WH
TU Delft Excellence Scholarships for International Students(Netherlands) https://www.tudelft.nl/en/education/practical-matters/scholarships/justus-louise-van-effen-excellence-scholarships/	EAP|EE|MENA|SCA|SSA|WH
Turkey Graduate Scholarships for International Students http://www.mfa.gov.tr/government-scholarships.en.mfa	EAP|EE|MENA|SCA|SSA|WH
TOWS/SIDA (The Organization of Women in Science for the Developing World) See also OWS https://owsd.net/career-development/phd-fellowship	EAP|EE|MENA|SCA|SSA|WH
UC International First Year Undergraduate Scholarships http://www.canterbury.ac.nz/scholarshipsearch/ScholarshipDetails.aspx?ScholarshipID=6935-1480	EAP|EE|MENA|SCA|SSA|WH
UEA International Development Scholarships for International Students (UK) https://www.uea.ac.uk/international-development/scholarships-and-funding/scholarships-international-students	EAP
UNCF Scholarships and Grants http://www.uncf.org/forstudents/scholarship.asp	EAP|EE|MENA|SCA|SSA|WH
UNESCO Fellowship Programmes: http://www.unesco.org/new/en/fellowships	EAP|EE|MENA|SCA|SSA|WH
• UNESCO/People's Republic of China (The Great Wall)	
• UNESCO/Czech Republic Co-Sponsored Fellowships	
• UNESCO/Poland Co-Sponsored Fellowships in Engineering	
• UNESCO/Poland Co-Sponsoed Fellowships in Archaeology and Conservation	
• UNESCO/Republic of Korea Co-Sponsored Fellowships	
• UNESCO/ISEDC (Russian Federation) Co-Sponsored Fellowships	
• UNESCO/Israel (Mashav) Co-Sponsored Fellowships	
• UNESCO/Sri Lanka Co-Sponsored Fellowships	
• UNESCO/L'OREAL Fellowships for Young Women in Life Sciences	
• UNESCO/Keizo Obuchi - Japan Young Researchers Fellowships	

Scholarship programs or providing/host organizations (continued)	World regions
UNIPV International Scholarships for Developing Countries http://www.unipv.eu/site/en/home/international-relations/cooperation-and-development/cicops-scholarships/articolo160.html	EAP|MENA|SCA|SSA|WH
United States–Timor Leste Scholarship Program: http://ustlscholarship.org/	SCA
United World Colleges (UWC) International Youth Scholarships: http://www.uwc.org/admissions	EAP|EE|MENA|SCA|SSA|WH
Università Cattolica International Scholarships http://www.ucscinternational.it/admission-at-ucsc/2-year-postgraduate-admissions/tuition-fees-and-scholarships-postgraduate-at-cattolica	EAP|EE|MENA|SCA|SSA|WH
Université de Lyon Master's Scholarships http://lyon-university.org/education/international-master-s-degrees-314154.kjsp?RH=PENstu	EAP|EE|MENA|SCA|SSA|WH
Université Paris-Saclay International Master's Scholarships https://www.universite-paris-saclay.fr/en/universite-paris-saclay-international-masters-scholarship-programme-academic-year-2017-2018	EAP|MENA|SCA|SSA|WH
University College London (UCL): http://www.ucl.ac.uk/prospective-students/scholarships	EAP|MENA|SCA|SSA|WH
University of Bern Masters Grants for International Students http://www.unibe.ch/studies/organizational_matters/student_financing/scholarships/index_eng.html	EAP|EE|MENA|SCA|SSA|WH
University of Bologna Study Grants for International Students http://www.unibo.it/en/services-and-opportunities/study-grants-and-subsidies/study-grants-for-international-students	EAP|EE|MENA|SCA|SSA|WH
University of Bradford Global Development Scholarships http://www.bradford.ac.uk/fees-and-financial-support/university-scholarships-and-support/info/global-development-scholarship-2017-18	EAP|EE|MENA|SCA|SSA|WH
University of Canterbury International First Year Scholarships (New Zealand) http://www.canterbury.ac.nz/future-students/fees-and-funding/scholarships-at-uc/	EAP|SCA|SSA
University of Essex Women of the Future Scholarships https://www1.essex.ac.uk/fees-and-funding/masters/scholarships/women-future.aspx	EAP|EE|MENA|SCA|SSA|WH
University of Geneva Excellence Masters Fellowships http://www.unige.ch/sciences/Enseignements/Formations/Masters/ExcellenceMasterFellowships_en.html	EAP|EE|MENA|SCA|SSA|WH
University of Hull International Office Postgraduate Scholarship http://www.hull.ac.uk/Choose-Hull/Study-at-Hull/Money/international-scholarships.aspx	EAP|MENA|SCA|SSA|WH
University of Lausanne Master's Grant for Foreign Students (Switzerland) https://www.unil.ch/international/en/home/menuguid/futures-etudiantes/bourses-master-de-lunil.html	EAP|EE|MENA|SCA|SSA|WH

Scholarship programs or providing/host organizations (continued)	World regions
University of Maastricht Scholarships for International students https://www.maastrichtuniversity.nl/support/your-studies-begin/coming-maastricht-university-abroad/scholarships	EAP|EE|MENA|SCA|SSA WH
University of Newcastle Postgraduate Research Scholarships https://www.newcastle.edu.au/research-and-innovation/graduate-research/phd-and-research-degrees/scholarships	EAP|EE|MENA|SCA|SSA WH
University of Otago Doctoral Scholarships (New Zealand) http://www.otago.ac.nz/study/scholarships/database/otago01687.html	EAP|EE|MENA|SCA|SSA WH
University of Oulu Tuition Fee Waivers for International Students http://www.oulu.fi/university/masters/scholarships	EAP|EE|MENA|SCA|SSA WH
UN-Nippon Fellowship Program in Ocean Affairs for Coastal Developing Countries http://www.un.org/depts/los/nippon/	EAP|EE|MENA|SCA|SSA WH
UNU-IIST PhD Scholarships for International Students (Macau) https://unu.edu/news/announcements/unu-iist-accepting-applications-for-floss-related-phd-scholarship.html	EAP|EE|MENA|SCA|SSA WH
UNU-INWEH Scholarships in Integrated Drylands Management for Developing Country Students http://inweh.unu.edu/msc-drylands/	EAP|EE|MENA|SCA|SSA WH
Uppsala IPK Scholarships for International Students (Sweden) https://www.uu.se/en/admissions/scholarships/uppsala-university/	EAP|EE|MENA|SCA|SSA WH
US Golf Association (USGA) Fellowship in Leadership and Service http://www.usga.org/aboutus/foundation/fellowship/fellowship.html	EAP|EE|MENA|SCA|SSA WH
Utrecht University Excellence Scholarships (Netherlands) https://www.uu.nl/masters/en/general-information/international-students/financial-matters/grants-and-scholarships/utrecht-excellence-scholarships	EAP|EE|MENA|SCA|SSA WH
UWE Bristol International Scholarship • Academic excellence scholarship • Country-specific scholarship • Millennium Scholarship • Justice Malek Ahmad Scholarship • Professor Arthur Li Scholarship • Master of Business Administration (MBA) • MSc International Management Scholarship • Faculty of Health and Applied Sciences MSc Scholarship www1.uwe.ac.uk/students/feesandfunding/fundingandscholarships/internationalstudentfunding.aspx	EAP|EE|MENA|SCA|SSA WH

Scholarship programs or providing/host organizations (end)	World regions
Vanier Canada Graduate Scholarships: www.vanier.gc.ca	EAP|EE|MENA|SCA|SSA|WH
Vice Chancellor's International Scholarship for Research Excellence at University of Nottingham http://www.nottingham.ac.uk/studywithus/international-applicants/scholarships-fees-and-finance/scholarships/research-scholarships/research-overseas.aspx	EAP|EE|MENA|SCA|SSA|WH
Vice-Chancellor's Excellence Scholarship at London South Bank University http://www.lsbu.ac.uk/courses/postgraduate/fees-and-funding/scholarships/vice-chancellor-scholarship	EAP|EE|MENA|SCA|SSA|WH
Vice-Chancellor's International Postgraduate Scholarships at University of Southern Queensland https://www.usq.edu.au/scholarships/usq/vice-chancellors-international-postgraduate	EAP|EE|MENA|SCA|SSA|WH
Vice-Chancellor's International Scholarships at University of the Arts London http://www.arts.ac.uk/study-at-ual/student-fees--funding/scholarships-search/ual-vice-chancellors-postgraduate-international-scholarships/	EAP|EE|MENA|SCA|SSA|WH
Villers Fellowship for Health Care Justice http://www.familiesusa.org/about/the-villers-fellowship.html	EAP|EE|MENA|SCA|SSA|WH
VLIR-UOS Scholarship Awards (Belgium): http://www.vliruos.be/en/scholarships/	EAP|EE|MENA|SCA|SSA|WH
Volkswagen Foundation: https://www.volkswagenstiftung.de/en/funding.html	EAP|EE|MENA|SCA|SSA|WH
VU University Amsterdam Fellowship Program (Netherlands) https://masters.vu.nl/en/international/scholarships/index.aspx	EAP|EE|MENA|SCA|SSA|WH
Warwick Chancellor's International Scholarships https://www2.warwick.ac.uk/fac/soc/pais/study/studyphd/funding/	EAP|EE|MENA|SCA|SSA|WH
Wellcome Trust Sanger Institute Vacation [Summer] Placements www.wellcome.ac.uk/Funding/Biomedical-science/Grants/Undergraduate-support/WTD004448.htm	EAP|EE|MENA|SCA|SSA|WH
Wells Mountain Foundation–International scholarships for students from developing http://www.wellsmountainfoundation.org/our-programs/scholarships/	EAP|MENA|SCA|SSA|WH
Wellstone Fellowship for Social Justice http://www.familiesusa.org/about/wellstone-fellowship.html	EAP|EE|MENA|SCA|SSA|WH
Wesleyan Freeman Scholarships for Asians: www.wesleyan.edu/admission/freeman	EAP|SCA
Wesleyan University Scholarships: http://www.wesleyan.edu/admission/informationfor/international.html	EAP|EE|MENA|SCA|SSA|WH
Westminster International Scholarships https://www.westminster.ac.uk/study/prospective-students/fees-and-funding/scholarships/international-postgraduate-scholarships	EAP|EE|MENA|SCA|SSA|WH
World Citizen Talent Scholarship for International Students (La Hague) https://www.thehagueuniversity.com/study-choice/admissions-and-finances/financing-your-bachelor-study/scholarships	EAP|EE|MENA|SCA|SSA|WH
World studio AIGA Scholarships http://www.worldstudio.org/schol/index.html	EAP|EE|MENA|SCA|SSA|WH

Appendix 4: good source for worldwide grade correspondence

Foreign Credits Inc
Foreign credits Inc's website has a very useful worldwide grade correspondence tool. Foreign Credits Inc. is an international verification, credential evaluation, and translation company:

www.foreigncredits.com/resources/grade-conversation/

Example: China vs USA

Grade Conversion

Country: China

Grading Scale: Five-Scale (Most common seco...

China

Scale	Description	U.S. Grade
90 - 100	优秀 (Excellent)	A
80 - 89	良好 (Good)	B
70 - 79	中等 (Satisfactory)	C
60 - 69	中等 / 及格 (Pass)	D
0 - 59	不及格 (Fail)	F

Tchetchet Gerard Digbohou has dedicated the last 11 years to successfully assisting students applying for schooling opportunities and scholarships outside of their country of residence. Over the years, he has built an in-depth knowledge of educational systems worldwide and has patiently compiled college admission and scholarship application best practices and has learned some of the best kept "secrets". His experience led him to put together CAPE, the 4-step approach to applying and winning scholarships for studies overseas described in his first book "The Secret To Winning an International Scholarship".

In 2003, as a student, Tchetchet was awarded the prestigious Fulbright scholarship which enabled him to pursue a fully funded Master's of Business Administration (MBA) in the United States. He is a graduate of the Middlebury Institute of International Studies at Monterey in California, USA and of the National Polytechnic Institute of Cote d'Ivoire.

A former Education USA advisor with the U.S. Department of State Bureau of Education, Tchetchet G. Digbohou is the cofounder of InterEdu Solutions an organization dedicated to helping students achieve their dreams of a better education and to the dissemination of best practices in higher education. He believes quality education should be available to everyone regardless of country of residence, socioeconomic status, or gender. He advocates for social empowerment and economic development and for the mobility of scholars worldwide.

THE SECRET TO WINNING AN INTERNATIONAL SCHOLARSHIP

THE COMPLETE GUIDE TO INTERNATIONAL SCHOLARSHIP APPLICATION

in 4 steps

First Edition